HAPPY TEAMS, SUCCESSFUL TEAMS

HAPPY TEAMS, SUCCESSFUL TEAMS

ROBINSON JOSEPH

© 2024 Robinson Joseph. All rights reserved.

No part of this publication may be reproduced, distributed, or transmitted in any form or by any means, including photocopying, recording, or other electronic or mechanical methods, without the prior written permission of the publisher, except in the case of brief quotations embodied in critical reviews and certain other noncommercial uses permitted by copyright law.

ISBN 979-8-3343-9657-9

TABLE OF CONTENTS

Author's Notes 9

CHAPTER 1
My Happiness and Productivity Reality Check 11

CHAPTER 2
The Pursuit of Happiness: Psychological Insights
and Workplace Implications 27

CHAPTER 3
The Science of Happiness 39

CHAPTER 4
Creating a Positive Work Environment or Circus 47

CHAPTER 5
Nurturing Employee Engagement and Satisfaction 59

CHAPTER 6
Enhancing Individual Happiness 83

CHAPTER 7
Overcoming Challenges of an Unhappy Workplace:
A Fun Guide to Boosting Productivity 95

CHAPTER 8
Successful Companies Embracing
Happiness to Improve Productivity 105

CHAPTER 9
Measuring Happiness in the Workplace 141

CHAPTER 10
The Critical Role of Happiness in the Workplace 149

Dedication

For my moms Sufrine and Mirta.
I hope you enjoy it as much as I do.

AUTHOR'S NOTE

As I pen down the final words of "Happy Teams, Successful Teams: The Power of a Happy Workplace," I am filled with immense gratitude for the individuals who have played a pivotal role in bringing this book to life. Their unwavering support, insights, and kick in the butt have been instrumental in shaping this work.

First and foremost, my heartfelt thanks go to Leenette. Your constant positivity and belief in this project have been a beacon of light throughout this journey. Your ability to find joy and spread happiness in the simplest of moments has been a true inspiration. Thank you for reminding me that happiness is indeed the cornerstone of productivity. Beso!

To Todd, I extend my deepest appreciation. Your sharp intellect and constructive feedback have been invaluable. Your ability to critically analyze and provide thoughtful suggestions has significantly enhanced the quality of this book. Thank you for your patience and for always pushing me to strive for excellence.

Finally, to Mark, your unwavering support and encouragement from day one have been a constant source of strength. Your optimism and steadfast belief in the message of this book have kept me motivated even during the toughest of times. Thank you for always being there for me and for believing in the vision of " Happy Teams, Successful Teams: The Power of a Happy Workplace".

This book is a testament to the power of collaboration and the incredible impact of having a supportive network. Leenette, Todd, and Mark, your contributions have been immeasurable, and I am forever grateful.

With deepest gratitude,
Rob Joseph

CHAPTER 1

HAPPINESS REALITY CHECK

I was fortunate enough to serve in the United States Air Force for over 30 years, 29 days, and 17 hours (but who is counting?). Beyond all the cool things we did, like defending our nation, traveling, and playing with cool toys, we thrived on camaraderie. We loved attending award dinners to support our teammates and fellow Airmen as they competed against each other. For those who have not served in the Armed Forces, our award dinners are like the Oscars, Emmys, or any other formal award event. However, unlike those fancy Hollywood events, we all wore clothes from the same designer: Uncle Sam.

I remember attending an awards dinner where the keynote speaker was a highly respected historical figure who'd previously served in the Air Force. He was a gifted speaker, and his speech was captivating, informative, and humorous. He embodied the type of presenter I admired. During his speech, he paused and asked the audience, "What do you believe to be truer? Happy people are productive people, or productive people are happy?" As a seasoned leader in the Air Force, I found this question to be a softball that I could knock out of the park. "Too easy, Mr. Highly Skilled Keynote Speaker," I thought to myself. I was so confident that I stood up and declared..." Happy People Are Productive People!"

Mr. Historical Air Force Man looked into my soul and said calmly that the correct answer was "Productive People Are Happy!" I looked around the room and was shocked to find most of my fellow service members nodding their heads in agreement. I was dumbfounded, in total disbelief that some people believed in productive people being happy more than in happy people being productive. How could I be wrong? How could I be so off-target on this ideology?

I stated earlier that I served in the Air Force for over 30 years. I have been a member of dozens of teams and managed dozens more directly. I thought of the successful teams and those that fell short, and I realized that it all came down to enjoying our workplace. Like most of us in the room, I'd had jobs that I dreaded going to. I remember working in the Post Office while going to college – a very well-paying job for any college kid. Now, you might envision me in a sky-blue polo and shorts, delivering mail or working the counter with a smile, asking if you'd like a book of stamps, but my role was far less glamorous. I was an environmental marshal. A facility maintainer. A sediment orderly. Or, to put it plainly, I was a janitor. I mopped, swept, dusted, painted, took out trash, and wrestled stuck mail from our machines. I was miserable. I hated going into the building and trying to be friendly to disgruntled workers who thought I was just a punk kid mopping the floor. My boss would instruct me on the day's tasks without lifting his head from his newspaper. There was no way I was going to stay there any longer. I was an intelligent kid working my way through college and I wanted to be treated like a person, not like an indentured servant. So, what did I do?! I dropped out of college and joined the Air Force!

Now I was in the Air Force! As a smart kid with some college under my belt and a few years on my peers, I felt I deserved some respect. I got to my first assignment and was welcomed by a team of coworkers excited to meet the new guy. The next day, I was scooped up from the barracks and taken to my unit, where I was introduced to my sergeant. She welcomed me with some humorous (let's say) non-Christian adjectives, which I found amusing. She was welcoming in.her unique own way. She informed me on the lunch time, who to contact if I needed a ride and gave me her personal number in case I ever needed her. Then she looked me in the eye and *asked* me to mop, sweep, dust, paint, take out the trash, and look for aircraft parts that may have fallen behind the shelves. I was ecstatic that I had found the respect and purpose I sought! How ironic that the same tasks I was doing at a better-paying job, which had driven me to quit everything, were now tasks I enjoyed doing so much more, even for less pay. I was happy to mop, dust, and paint like there was no tomorrow, and I did it with a smile!

We've all heard of companies incorporating unconventional methods in their organizational structure. Well-known companies like Facebook, Google, Apple, Zappos, and GAP have long since abandoned the suit and tie (or pencil skirt) persona. Now they embrace T-shirts, cargo shorts, and whatever makes you comfortable, with no cubicles in sight and unlimited snacks and drinks. Some of these companies have invested millions of dollars to modernize their facilities' decor and other physical features. They are no longer housed in buildings, but entire campuses. It's not uncommon for a team at Facebook or Progressive Insurance to hold a critical personnel meeting at the courtyard, lawn, or some other offbeat setting, possibly having a cappuccino with Flo or that little redhead guy who does everything.

Why? Why the sudden shift away from what had been the norm for so long? Don't Google and Apple have plenty of money to pay Mr. Smith or Ms. Jones enough to be happy and productive? Why do they need to do the "extra"? At the end of the day, isn't it all about that bottom dollar? These companies are trying to make their workplace more enticing and, more importantly, more conducive to production.

When I was retiring, I heard the same thing a dozen different ways from my colleagues:

"Are you going to work for Google?"

"Go to Amazon!"

"Go to Facebook."

"You should work for so and so!"

I felt like Morgan Freeman leaving the prison in *Shawshank Redemption*, where everyone had an opinion on what he should do because they either didn't have the opportunity or just craved it. As lax as some may say the Air Force is, we do have a rigid military structure. I think my friends just wanted me to experience an organization that was very different from what we had experienced throughout our Air Force careers so they could live vicariously through me.

The fascinating thing about companies redefining the workplace is that they overlook the most important asset a business may have: its people. Out of all the companies I mentioned – Facebook, Google, Apple and Progressive Insurance – how many do you think made the top 10 of *Fortune's 100 Best Companies To Work For*? What about the top 25? The top 50? How many even made the list at all? Surprisingly, only Progressive Insurance did, coming in at #49.

I'm not saying that these companies aren't excellent places to work, but they didn't make the top 100. It takes more than removing cubicles, installing a smoothie bar, or Flip Flop Fridays to ensure employees enjoy coming to work. When Fortune Magazine released its 2020 100 *Best Companies To Work For* list, I scanned the list and reviewed the common attributes employees mentioned. Not once did words like "office decoration," "workstations," or "unlimited snacks" appear. Of course, the word "benefits" came up a few times. Still, the more prominent words that appeared in every company's evaluation were words like *love, leadership, members, family, care, and everyone*. The word *people* was the most consistent top indicator.

The #1 best company to work for, according to Fortune, was Hilton. When surveyed, 97% of Hilton employees said they felt welcomed when they joined the company. Hilton has over 62,000 employees and over 6100 properties across the globe. To achieve such high employee satisfaction is no small feat, especially considering they have employees everywhere from Tennessee to Tanzania.

Ultimate Technology, ranked #2 in 2020, saw 98% of their nearly 6000 employees say they were "proud to tell people they work there." All of the top 100 companies had high marks for statements like:

- "I can take time off when necessary."
- "I feel good about the ways we contribute to the community." or,
- "People here are given lots of responsibilities."

It was evident to me that most of the factors that made people happy at work were not the pay or stock options but the soft skills and interaction with coworkers, colleagues, and customers.

When I worked at the Post Office, I hated my job. I dreaded the commute and every night before going to work, I hoped that a few people would call in sick or that certain individuals weren't on the schedule or were on vacation. I told you that I enjoyed my first assignment in the Air Force, and I do mean that. But keep in mind, during my Air Force career, I had 14 assignments all over the world and a handful of deployments (you know, those extended periods in locations like Iraq or Afghanistan). At some point during those assignments or deployments, I felt like that 18-year-old working at the Post Office again. I hated coming to work. I hoped Sgt. So-and-So was on vacation or I that I wouldn't run into John Doe, believing their absence would make my day better. When I did get to the workplace and Sgt. So-and-So or Postmaster What's-His-Name was there, I just wasn't myself. I wasn't the same driven or motivated individual. I knew for a fact that my performance suffered on those days. I can do a pretty good job under most stressful conditions, but because I wasn't "happy," I know I left some in the tank or stepped off the gas.

If I were to canvass an audience and ask, "Have you ever worked in a place where you were not happy?" I am confident that most of you would say yes. Those who said no probably had only one job or were just plain lucky. Unhappy workers tend to exhibit some common attributes we can all recognize. I read a book by S. Chris Edmonds called *The Culture Engine*, where he listed some tell-tale signs of an unhappy coworker. I want to elaborate on some of them that resonated with me.

- **Complaining More Often:** Many of us can walk into an establishment and immediately point out the unhappy employee. If you can't, don't worry, they'll likely tell you. Whether you are a colleague or a customer, unhappy employees are some of the most vocal people you can encounter. They might say things like, "Why is HR asking us to attend this training?" or "I can't believe they are asking us to do this." Even as a customer, you might hear, "I can't wait to get off of work, I haven't had a day off in a week," or "I hope your day is going better than mine." More effort is placed into being counterproductive than being productive.

- **Minimal Effort:** An unhappy employee is unlikely to go the extra mile. They may do just enough to not get fired. I remember a time when my family would get the latest news from a teenager on a bike who would throw the morning paper onto our porch every day. I could always tell when something was bothering him. It's not like I would get up at 6 AM and ask him, but I noticed that when he was not in a good mood, our paper would end up in the bushes, by the side of the house, or on the roof.

  On those days when he seemed to enjoy his job, he would toss the newspaper as if he were playing catch with a toddler, with accuracy and grace. Too often, though, he would come as the News Ninja, trying to decapitate the garden gnomes my wife placed in the front. He would do the bare minimum to get our paper to our house. Eventually, we canceled our subscription and went elsewhere for our news. Imagine how many more subscriptions my hometown paper could have had if the paperboy had done more than the bare minimum. At the Post Office, I would collect trash in the receptacles once or maybe twice a day. If it happened to get filled after my collection, I would purposely ignore it for the next shift. Sadly I, too, only did the minimum of what was expected.

- **More Mistakes:** Have you pulled over after going through a drive-thru to carefully inspect your entire order, thereby defeating the purpose of "fast-food"? I have a beautiful daughter who, as a teenager, worked for a fast-food chain that would hire high school students during the summer. Like most teenagers, they hated workdays but loved paydays.

  My daughter would come home and pout about how she hated smelling like fries or wearing this ugly uniform, or how she could not believe she had to work this weekend while her friends went to the shore. She would then complain about customers being upset that she had messed up their order. I told her that her attitude towards work reflected in her performance. Unhappy employees make more mistakes because they do not fully apply themselves. Like most unhappy employees, my daughter made mistakes because she did not care.

- **Lack of Participation:** We all know disgruntled Dan from R&D and angry Amy from HR won't be at the company holiday party or any after-hours functions. You can look around the room at any team building event and the unhappy employees are usually the ones that are either absent or distant.
- **Excitement About Leaving:** Unhappy employees tend to hit the snooze button harder than their happy counterparts and are more excited about leaving work than arriving. They have an internal coach that is hard at work, motivating them with thoughts like "We have five more days until the weekend!" or, "Try not to cuss him out." When it's finally time to leave, they are the first to log off or have their timecard ready in-hand like a boarding pass.
- **Quitting:** Employee retention is critical for successful businesses. Most people who quit their jobs are unhappy about something. Consider the time, resources, and money that go into training a new employee. Productivity slows as existing staff help the latest addition, and mistakes can be costly if your trainee quits after a month with the company. While serving in the Air Force, I made a conscious effort to engage with new members. I knew not everyone planned to make it a long career like I did, but every member planned on doing at least four years of service.

When Airmen reached the crossroads of either leaving the Air Force or committing to another term, I sat with them to discuss why. If they decided to stay, then the conversation was brief, and I closed with, "Thanks for reenlisting. Now get your butt out of my office". If they decided not to reenlist or complete their term of service, I had a series of questions as to why and what we could have done as an organization or service to have encouraged them to reenlist. Most of the time, it was because they wanted to pursue outside opportunities or had a job offer due to the skills they acquired. In the rare instance when I encounter a member who was completely unhappy with their role, I tried to understand the details of their unhappiness and explore avenues to keep them serving. I knew it cost more than $60,000 to train each Airman, and depending on their specialty, it might cost even more. Once the reason for their exit was determined, I still ended with my usual pleasantry of "Thank you for serving our great nation. Now get your butt out of my office."

- **Quiet Quitting:** Even worse than quitting and leaving is when employees quit and then stay. Unhappy employees may take the low road, mentally checking out and opting to do less than the minimum. In the Air Force, we called this going ROAD: "**R**etired **O**n **A**ctive **D**uty. Unhappiness is more evident when a high performer has a drastic drop in performance. Due to their solid track record, we tended to allow them to ride their low for an extended period without addressing the root cause of their lack of productivity.

You may be wondering, then, what is happiness in the workplace? Does it mean having candy and ice cream in the break room? Complimentary tickets to your favorite sports team's games? Free pony rides in the employee parking lot or a musical set by our favorite singer/band? While some of these scenarios may bring happiness to individuals (well, at least me), they don't necessarily apply to every employee. You can't implement the Golden Rule as a rule of law in your organization. As incredible as it may sound to "Treat others the way you want to be treated," it doesn't always work in practice. For example, I would be pretty unhappy if you offered me ice cream because you happen to love mint chocolate. Not only do I find mint chocolate disgusting, but I am also lactose intolerant and would likely think you are out to get me.

Instituting an employee treatment policy based on the Platinum Rule would bring you much closer to the goal of happier employees. The Platinum Rule is simple: "Treat people the way they want to be treated." Organizations using this rule gain a better understanding of their employees' needs and preferences. Some people don't want ponies in the parking lot because ponies leave pony poop and Robinson, who has no willpower to ice cream, will end up spending more time in the bathroom than an attendee of a Lamaze class. Listening to and understanding your employees is essential to promoting a happy work environment.

There was a time in the Air Force when I was leading a team of over hundreds of men and women. In the Air Force, everyone is a salaried employee so there was no way to monetarily incentivize good work. I had to find other ways to promote enhanced production. I initially tried to lead using the Golden Rule method. I used to allow people to get off work early if a particular task was accomplished. I loved getting off work early; it allowed me to run some errands, pick up my kids from school, and start dinner. But even with the early release perk, I realized that not everyone on my team was working to their full potential. After a few attempts, I held a team meeting and asked if they were happy with getting off early. Most were delighted, but as I scanned the crowd, I noticed a few instances of non-verbal displeasure. I asked one individual, and she hesitantly said, "Chief, getting off work is great, but my husband and I only have one car, so he has to take time off work to come to pick me up, and he is losing the extra hours we need to make ends meet." Another sergeant came to me and said, "Chief, I would rather have an extra hour for lunch than get off early so I can have lunch with my child in school." I thought everyone wanted to get off early because I was using the Golden Rule instead of applying the Platinum Rule to find a way to incentivize on an individual basis.

Understanding and knowing your employees is what makes them happy. Employees want to feel that they matter, that they are appreciated and valued. They want to feel engaged and, perhaps most importantly, that they work in a positive workplace culture. When I was at the Post Office, I felt like a loner with a mop or broom. In contrast, when I joined the Air Force, I felt like I was part of a team, even if I just happened to be holding the mop or the broom.

I knew that happy people make productive people because I had seen it so many times in the units I worked in. As an immature leader, I used to say to my subordinates, "I don't care if you are happy or not. We have a job to do, and you are getting paid on the 1st and the 15th to do it!" That approach only resulted in average production from the teams I led. The University of Warwick study show that happy employees are 12-20% more productive than unhappy employees. For those of you who are in sales, the same research shows that sales rose 37% with happy salespeople. Organizations are now taking a closer look at the effects of happy people in their workplace. What is not surprising is that the stock prices of *Fortune's 100 Best Companies to Work For* rose an average of 14% per year since 2004, while companies not on the list only reported a 6% increase. Now you see why companies are trying to crack the formula of having happy employees.

Happy employees provide more than just the bottom dollar for companies. They tend to care more about the organization, the product or service that is being provided, and the people in the organization. Happy employees care about how their company is viewed, and in today's social media-laden world, that is important.

Happy employees are more attuned to what is going on both inside and outside the company. A happy person would be the first to know when someone isn't happy. If I, being happy, spoke to Disgruntled Dan in the cafeteria or during a meeting, I could quickly tell he was not satisfied with something in the organization. Why isn't he as excited about the merger as I am? How come when I mentioned our section lead, he didn't concur? Why did he roll his eyes when I brought up someone's name? Happy people tend to want others to be happy too; no one wants to work with a Debbie Downer.

Happy people are some of the most loyal employees you may have. They have a vested interest in making the company, team, or project succeed. We spoke on retention earlier, but I just want to emphasize that loyal employees stay longer in an organization. The Bureau of Labor Statistics show on average, an employee stays with a company is for 3.2 years, and if they are in management, 5.5 years. High retention rates mean less turnover, less time spent training new hires, and less time and money spent trying to replace skilled personnel. Gone are the days when employees were hired right out of high school or college and stayed until they could nab their retirement gold watch and ride off into the sunset.

Loyalty goes beyond retention. In the Air Force, duty hours were a bit flexible. As salaried employees, we received the same pay regardless of the number of hours worked. It was not uncommon for a hot task to come down just before the end of the workday, requiring extra hours. Sometimes, I would ask an individual if they could stay an hour or two later to help. Since I was in charge, most felt obligated or pressured to stay, which was fine by me. I realized that the members who were happy and loyal to the team, organization, or even to me, had no qualms whatsoever and were enthusiastic about helping. The unhappy ones, however, provided minimal effort and watched the clock closely, just waiting for when their extra hour was up. Having loyal, happy employees is essential to the survival and performance of any company.

Another benefit of having happy people on your team is the innovation they bring. Happy employees vested in the company tend to find new ways to improve processes or products. They strive to make their team better. Happy people tend to feel freer and more comfortable to express their thoughts and ideas, which allows the company to produce more efficient or creative products or services.

Happiness is contagious. Happy people make happy teams, who in turn make happy bosses, who then make more happy people, and the cycle continues. How simple is that? Do you ever wonder why those in-person interviews are so important? Are you compatible with our happy team? Freelance writer Gerald Ainomugisha stated, "Happiness increases productivity because happy employees support one other." When employees have positive attitudes, they are more willing to help fellow workers achieve the company's goals, especially in group projects. Happy employees are also more likely to ask for help when they need it, which is crucial for productivity. Many employees feel ashamed or embarrassed to ask for support due to the fear of being viewed as incompetent.

The happier the employees are, the healthier they are. Unhappy employees are burdened with job-related stress and anxiety. This day-to-day strain leads to psychological injuries, negatively affecting the immune system. Unhappy people tend to call out sick more often than happy people, sometimes just to get mental relief from their workplace. Depressed workers take 20 times more sick days per month, leaving your company shorthanded more often. Happy people keep your organization flowing with vitality and liveliness.

I was a Chief Master Sergeant in the United States Air Force, in the top 1 percent of the enlisted corps as mandated by federal law. I had the positional and legal power to issue directives to be executed. In other words, I was kind of a big deal. Despite all the pompous glory and assumed authority, I could not order someone to change their emotional state. You know how, when you were young and crying, your parents would yell, "Stop that crying!" and you would try your hardest to instantly dry those tears and catch your breath, which was impossible? Similarly, I could not order everyone in my organization to be happy. Much like that parent with a crying child, I had to find a different approach: I used HAPPY to foster happy employees.

I decided the best way to foster a happy workplace is to break down the word "happy" into an easy-to-remember tool: **H**onestly **A**ssessing **P**urpose, **P**eople, and **Y**ourself. To ensure I made decisions with the least negative impact on overall happiness, I would first honestly assess the purpose. Why do I need to implement this new policy? What is the purpose of producing this product? Who or what does it benefit? By clearly understanding the purpose of our actions, I could better relay it to those involved and gain one of the most essential support factors: "buy-in." If my employees bought in to what we were doing, reaching our goal became more attainable. For example, I would be thrilled to make widgets all day if I knew they were being used in equipment to fight cancer or in a new vehicle model because I bought into that purpose. But if we were making widgets to be added to clubs to bludgeon baby seals, I would not be too happy about that.

It is not very often that someone joins an organization intending to do a lousy job. People seek employment for various reasons, the most obvious being money. They need to pay on their student loans, make rent, support their family, or maybe pay off a loan shark named Louie from Joyzee. To make more money, individuals know they must perform at a certain level to potentially receive raises or bonuses. If someone is not performing to a certain level, are we giving them all they need to succeed? Are we providing enough training? Do we have the right tools? Is there something outside the organization we are not considering? Have we provided a safe work environment? Do we have a mechanism in place that offers a means to complain or address problems in the organization?

In the Air Force, commanders brief their organizations that they have an open-door policy. "My door is always open if you ever have anything you want to talk about or address." Little did they know it was like an American Ninja Warrior gauntlet to get to that door. The obstacles are informing your immediate supervisor, then middle management, then the commander's executive, then the chief, and finally, you get to the commander, who asks you, "Did you inform your supervisor?" Nothing brings down morale or takes the wind out of an individual's sails more than the inability to voice concerns. I tell folks that problems or issues you are facing are like wet laundry in the washing machine—the longer you take to air it out, the worse it gets.

Lastly, you should honestly assess yourself. It is hard to be critical of your own decisions, but sometimes you have to take a step back and see if you are the cause of the unhappiness. I remember being on the staff of a senior military officer. He had been on the job for three months and called me into his office. He then asked me how he was doing. How was he being perceived by the rest of the staff? Was he doing a good job so far? I was taken aback by the range of questions. I was in the presence of a high-ranking official who had commanded numerous times, and he asked me how he was doing. To the ladies in the audience, I am sure you have realized that there are three things that are hard for a man to ask for, and they all start with the letter 'F': funds, feedback, and, of course, forgiveness. Giving honest feedback to him at that moment was not only crucial for the organization moving forward but also for his professional growth. If you are leading a team, it is critical to get that feedback. If any of you have attended a Giant Worldwide leadership training, they emphasize "know yourself to lead yourself" and "You cannot give what you don't possess." So, if you can lead yourself, you can lead others.

All of this is why happy people are productive people, and not the other way around. In the mid-1800s, there was a farmer who was the richest in his industry. He had one of the largest workforces at that time, with over 850 workers. He was worth 3.5 million dollars. Even for today's standard $3.5 million makes a farmer very successful. However, $3.5 million in the mid-1800s is valued at nearly $120 million today. No doubt he was very productive. Sadly, the 850 workers were enslaved men, women, and children. Highly productive, yes, but I can assure you that they were not very happy.

I can slightly see why Mr. Big Time Air Force keynote speaker might think that productive people being happy is more accurate, because I do know some folks are ecstatic when they are productive or deeply immersed in a project. Unlike the "what came first, the chicken or the egg" analogy, it is clear that you would not be ecstatic about being productive if you were not happy in the first place. So, let's jump into the reasoning why I firmly believe happy teams make successful teams.

CHAPTER 2

THE PURSUIT OF HAPPINESS: PSYCHOLOGICAL INSIGHTS AND WORKPLACE IMPLICATIONS

Ah, happiness! The elusive butterfly we all chase, the unicorn of emotions, the Bigfoot of our inner world. We all want it, but do we really know what it is? Why didn't you laugh at my joke? Why do some events bring me happiness and not you? Let's embark on this joyous journey together and unravel the mystery of what happiness truly is.

The Great Happiness Hunt

Imagine you're on a safari, not in the wilds of Africa but in the savannah of your mind. Your goal? To catch a glimpse of the rare and majestic Happiness. As you trudge through the thick foliage of daily life, dodging the quicksand of bills, responsibilities, your spouse's "honey-do" lists, and the prickly bushes of social media drama, you might wonder, "Is happiness even real, or just a legend?"

Happiness: The Mythical Creature

Some say happiness is a constant state of euphoria, a never-ending parade of rainbows, puppies, and a nice glass of your favorite aged beverage. But if we were always euphoric, our faces would hurt from smiling, and we'd never get anything done. Imagine filing taxes while riding a unicorn on a sugar high. Not very practical, right?

Others claim happiness is a serene lake of calm where you float peacefully without a care in the world. This sounds lovely until you realize that floating too long makes you prune up, and you might get sunburned, and you have to get to shore to pick up the kid from daycare. Plus, where did all these mosquitos and other bugs come from?!

The Science of Smiles

Let's get a bit scientific here. According to those lab coat-wearing folks, happiness is a cocktail of brain chemicals: dopamine, serotonin, endorphins, and oxytocin. Picture your brain as a bar; these chemicals are the mixologists, shaking up delightful concoctions. Sometimes, they nail the perfect blend, and you feel on top of the world. Other times, one of them goes on a break, and you're left with a flat soda of a mood.

But remember, even scientists can't agree on what exactly happiness is. They poke, prod, and measure, and yet nailing down what happiness is about as easy as nailing Jell-O to a wall or weighing a cloud on a kitchen scale.

The Pursuit of Happiness

I'm sure you've heard of the pursuit of happiness. It's enshrined in the Declaration of Independence, right between life and liberty. But pursuing happiness can sometimes feel like chasing your own shadow. The faster you run, the more it eludes you.

Here's a plot twist: happiness often finds you when you're not looking for it. It sneaks up on you while you're doing something else, like helping a friend move (even though you swore you'd never do it again after the last time) or getting lost in a good book. Those little moments catch you off guard, like finding twenty bucks in an old coat pocket.

In the quest to define happiness, psychology presents it as more than a fleeting emotion or a mere absence of sadness. From a psychological perspective, happiness is often divided into two main components: hedonic and eudaimonic. Hedonic happiness is derived from pleasure or the avoidance of pain, emphasizing immediate gratification and sensory delight. In contrast, eudaimonic happiness is associated with living by one's true self, achieving personal growth, and realizing one's potential. This distinction is crucial for understanding happiness's role and implications in the workplace. We will explore the science of happiness in Chapter 2.

The Psychology of Happiness

Modern psychological research has sought to measure and understand the factors contributing to happiness. According to Positive Psychology, the scientific study of what makes life most worth living, happiness is part of broader constructs like well-being and life satisfaction. Key factors contributing to happiness include positive relationships, meaningful work, engagement, accomplishments, and the cultivation of positive emotions and resilience.

The PERMA model, proposed by psychologist Martin Seligman, encapsulates these factors into five core elements of psychological well-being and happiness: **Positive Emotions**, **Engagement**, **Rela-**

tionships, **M**eaning, and **A**ccomplishments. Each component plays a critical role in nurturing an individual's well-being, offering a framework that can be applied in various aspects of life, including the workplace.

The PERMA model identifies five core elements that contribute to a fulfilling and meaningful life:

1. **Positive Emotions (P):** This aspect of well-being involves experiencing positive emotions such as joy, gratitude, satisfaction, and contentment. Positive emotions broaden our perspective, enhance creativity, and build psychological resilience.
2. **Engagement (E):** Also referred to as "flow," engagement refers to being fully absorbed and immersed in activities that challenge and stretch our skills. When engaged in activities we enjoy and find meaningful, we experience a sense of timelessness and deep concentration.
3. **Relationships (R):** Social connections and supportive relationships are vital for well-being. Positive relationships with friends, family, colleagues, and community members provide emotional support, a sense of belonging, and opportunities for growth and connection.
4. **Meaning (M):** Having a sense of purpose and meaning in life is essential for well-being. Meaning can be derived from personal values, goals, beliefs, and contributing to something greater than oneself, such as family, work, community, or spirituality.
5. **Accomplishments (A):** Achieving goals and accomplishments, both big and small, contributes to a sense of competence, mastery, and self-efficacy. Setting and pursuing meaningful goals provides direction, motivation, and a sense of achievement.

The PERMA model suggests that a combination of these five elements—positive emotion, engagement, relationships, meaning, and accomplishment—leads to greater overall well-being and happiness. Seligman proposed that focusing on these elements can help individuals flourish and lead more fulfilling lives.

The Happiness Pie

In another study, Psychologist Sonja Lyubomirsky argued that happiness is like a pie. According to the "happiness pie chart," about 50% of your happiness is determined by your genetics—your personal "happiness set point." Think of it as the size of your pie tin. Some folks have a family-sized tin, while others have one just big enough for a cupcake.

Another 10% is circumstances—your job, your relationships, whether your favorite team won last night's game. We often focus on this part the most, thinking a new car or a vacation will fill our happiness pie. But, alas, it's just a sliver.

The remaining 40%? That's up to you, my friend. It's your thoughts, actions, and attitudes – the secret recipe you concoct in your kitchen. You can add a scoop of gratitude, a sprinkle of kindness, and maybe even a dash of humor (highly recommended).

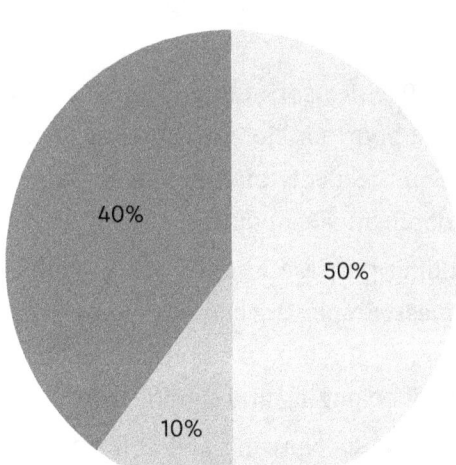

Happiness Pie Chart

● Genetics ● Circumstances ● Thoughts, Actions, and Attitudes

Happiness in the Workplace

The implications of happiness in the workplace extend far beyond mere job satisfaction. A happy workforce is often more productive, creative, and committed. Employers and managers, therefore, have a vested interest in fostering an environment that promotes the well-being and happiness of their employees. This involves creating a culture that values and supports the psychological drivers of happiness.

1. **Positive Emotions:** Cultivating a positive work environment that encourages joy, gratitude, and optimism can boost morale and productivity. This can be achieved through recognition programs, team-building activities, and an overall positive communication culture.
2. **Engagement:** Employees are more likely to be happy when they are deeply engaged with their work. This involves tasks challenging them without causing undue stress, opportunities for flow experiences, and roles aligning with their skills and interests.
3. **Relationships:** Positive social connections at work are crucial for emotional support and job satisfaction. Fostering a culture of collaboration, respect, and kindness can enhance team dynamics and individual happiness.
4. **Meaning:** Finding purpose in one's work significantly contributes to happiness. Employers can help employees see how their roles contribute to the organization's larger mission, thus providing a sense of belonging and significance.
5. **Accomplishments:** Recognizing and celebrating achievements, both big and small, boosts confidence and reinforces a sense of progress and efficacy. Goal setting and feedback are essential processes in this regard.

Implementing Happiness Strategies

A multifaceted approach is necessary for organizations seeking to enhance happiness and well-being. This includes assessing and improving the work environment, leadership styles, job roles, and the overall organizational culture. Surveys and regular check-ins can provide insights into employee needs and happiness levels, guiding targeted interventions.

Moreover, personal development programs focusing on strengths rather than weaknesses, mindfulness and resilience training, and flexible work arrangements can contribute significantly to employee happiness.

Understanding happiness from a psychological perspective offers valuable insights into its complex nature and the factors that foster it. In the workplace, where individuals spend a considerable portion of their lives, the implications of happiness are profound. By adopting a holistic approach that addresses the various components of happiness, organizations can unlock the full potential of their workforce, leading to enhanced well-being, productivity, and success. The journey toward personal and professional happiness is an ongoing process of discovery, adaptation, and growth.

The Happiness and Productivity Connection

In today's fast-paced and competitive work environments, productivity often takes center stage. However, recent research has shed light on a crucial factor that can significantly impact productivity: happiness. We explore the intricate link between happiness and productivity, drawing on empirical evidence and real-world examples to illustrate the profound implications of fostering happiness in the workplace.

Understanding the Relationship

Numerous studies have investigated the relationship between happiness and productivity, consistently finding a positive correlation between the two. One seminal study by researchers at the University of Warwick found that happy employees were 12% more productive than their unhappy counterparts. Subsequent research across various industries and organizational settings has corroborated this finding.

Research Findings

1. **Positive Emotions and Cognitive Performance:** Psychological research has demonstrated positive emotions enhance cognitive performance. A study published in the *Journal of Experimental Psychology: General* found that individuals experiencing positive emotions demonstrated greater creativity and problem-solving abilities. This suggests that happiness can directly influence cognitive processes, leading to improved productivity in tasks requiring innovation and critical thinking.

2. **Motivation and Engagement:** Happiness is closely linked to motivation and engagement in the workplace. A meta-analysis published in the *Journal of Applied Psychology* revealed a significant positive relationship between employee satisfaction

and job performance. Happy employees exhibit higher levels of enthusiasm, commitment, and effort in their work, resulting in increased productivity and performance.

3. **Resilience and Stress Management:** Happiness is associated with greater resilience and practical stress management skills. Research conducted by the American Psychological Association found that individuals with higher levels of subjective well-being were better able to cope with work-related stressors and recover from setbacks. This resilience translates into higher productivity levels, as happy employees are less likely to experience burnout or absenteeism.

Happiness in Perspective

Finally, let's put happiness in perspective. It's not about being in a perpetual state of bliss. That's just not realistic. Life has ups and downs, twists and turns. Sometimes, happiness is just a quiet contentment, a feeling of peace amidst the chaos.

Think of happiness as a trusty sidekick, not the hero of your story. It's there to support you, lighten your load, and give you a wink and a nudge when you need it most. It's not about having everything you want but appreciating what you have.

Happiness Hacks

Since we all love a good hack, here are some tried-and-true tricks of the trade to nudge that happiness meter:

1. **Laugh at Yourself:** If you can't laugh at yourself, you're missing out on the best comedy show in town. Embrace your quirks and foibles. Trip over your own feet? Just call it a new TikTok or interpretive dance.
2. **Practice Gratitude:** Yes, it's cliché, but counting your blessings really works. Start small – be thankful for that cup of coffee that didn't spill on your shirt this morning or that you even woke up this morning.
3. **Get Moving:** Exercise releases those happy chemicals we talked about. Plus, it gives you an excuse to wear those fancy workout clothes you bought and to pose in the mirror.
4. **Connect with Others:** Humans are social creatures by nature. Even introverts need some social interaction. Just make sure it's with people who lift you, not ones who drain your soul. Find folks that Call You Up and not Call You Out. (Special thanks to Mark and Todd)
5. **Do Something Nice:** Acts of kindness make us feel good. Hold the door for someone (even if they don't say thank you), compliment a stranger, or buy a coffee for the person behind you in line. It's an instant mood booster.

In the grand safari of life, happiness isn't the destination – the goofy, unpredictable, and sometimes elusive companion makes the journey worthwhile. So, keep your eyes open, your heart light, and your sense of humor intact. Happiness is out there, waiting to be discovered in the most unexpected places, especially in the workplace.

And remember, if all else fails, there's always chocolate and aged beverages.

Reflection Questions

How do you personally define happiness and productivity?

In what ways do your definitions align or differ from conventional definitions?

How do happiness and productivity influence each other?

Can productivity be sustained in the absence of happiness? Conversely, can happiness be maintained without productivity?

How do short-term gains in productivity impact long-term happiness?

Are there scenarios where short-term happiness leads to long-term productivity gains?

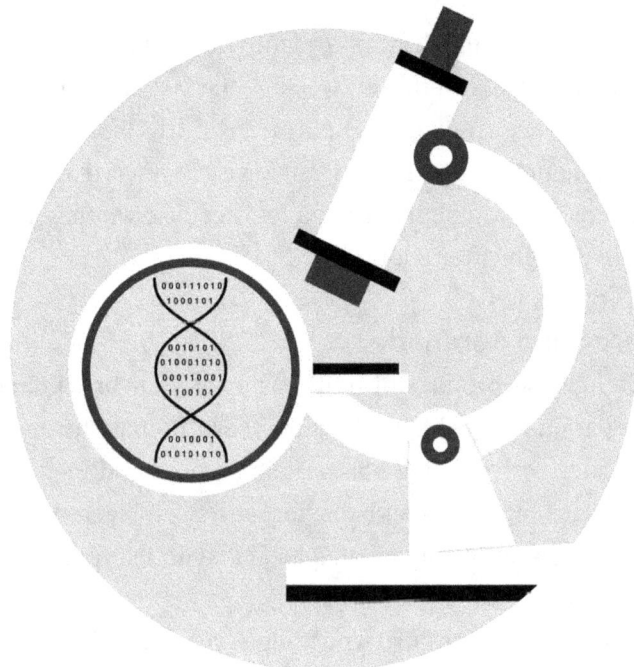

CHAPTER 3

THE SCIENCE OF HAPPINESS

Ever wonder if you can scientifically analyze happiness? Spoiler alert: You can! Welcome to the whimsical world of happiness science, where joy meets jargon and giggles meet graphs.

The Dopamine Dance

First stop: your brain's very own party planner, dopamine. Dopamine is that friend who always knows the best clubs and keeps the energy high. When you do something pleasurable, like eating your favorite ice cream or getting Wi-Fi on a plane, dopamine is released. It's your brain saying, "Hey, this is awesome. Let's do it again!"

Scientists have studied this neurotransmitter like detectives on a stakeout, figuring out it's heavily involved in reward and pleasure mechanisms. Dopamine makes you feel ecstatic when you see the pizza delivery guy after a long day.

The Serotonin Serenade

Next, we have serotonin, the zen master of your brain chemicals. While dopamine is the life of the party, serotonin is the one sitting in the corner with reading glasses, sipping tea and meditating. It helps regulate mood, social behavior, and even sleep. When your serotonin levels are balanced, you feel calm and content, like a cat in a sunbeam.

Serotonin is the wise guru who nudges you towards mindfulness and gratitude. It's why you feel serene joy when you watch a beautiful sunset or your newborn baby does something adorable. And yes, scientists have poked and prodded at serotonin enough to know it's crucial for avoiding the dark pit of despair.

Endorphins: The Natural High

Endorphins are the body's little stash of opiates. They're released during activities like exercise, laughter, and even spicy food consumption. Ever heard of a "runner's high"? That's endorphins doing their happy dance, making you feel invincible after a good jog or, let's be honest, a brisk walk to the beer fridge (I don't judge).

Picture endorphins as tiny cheerleaders, boosting your mood and numbing pain. They're the reason people say, "Laughter is the best medicine." So next time you laugh so hard you cry, remember: you're self-medicating with joy.

Oxytocin: The Hug Hormone

Let's talk about oxytocin, often dubbed the "love hormone." Released during bonding moments like hugging, cuddling, holding hands, or even making eye contact, oxytocin is why social connections feel so darn good. It's not just about romantic love, either–oxytocin is all about social bonding and trust.

Scientists have discovered that oxytocin increases trust and empathy. So, it's not just warm fuzzies; it's a full-blown cuddle-fest in your brain. Oxytocin is your inner hippie, promoting peace, love, and understanding while reducing stress and anxiety. It's why petting a dog or receiving a genuine compliment can make your day.

Philosophy and Psychology of Happiness

Happiness is a complex emotional state characterized by joy, satisfaction, contentment, and fulfillment. While happiness has many facets and can be understood in various ways, it generally involves positive emotions and life experiences.

Philosophically, happiness is considered in terms of living a good life or flourishing rather than simply being an emotion. In this broader sense, happiness is related to the pursuit of meaning, purpose, and personal growth.

Psychologically, happiness can be analyzed into more specific states, such as pleasure, a sense of achievement, or emotional well-being. Research often distinguishes between two types of happiness:

1. **Hedonic happiness (or pleasure)** involves immediate gratification or enjoyment arising from experiences like eating a favorite food, enjoying a party, or relaxing in a comfortable environment.
2. **Eudaimonic happiness** comes from engaging in meaningful activities or pursuing long-term goals that lead to a sense of ful-

fillment, such as building a successful career, nurturing a family, or contributing to the community.

Different cultures and individuals may prioritize these aspects differently, and what makes one person happy might not necessarily work for someone else. Factors contributing to happiness include genetics, life circumstances, achievements, marital status, social relationships, financial security, mental and physical health, and overall lifestyle choices.

In the pursuit of understanding happiness, scientists have delved into various fields of study, uncovering intricate connections between our thoughts, behaviors, and biology. One such branch of psychology that has contributed significantly to our comprehension of happiness is Positive Psychology. Moreover, advances in neurobiology have shed light on the intricate workings of the brain, offering insights into the physiological mechanisms underlying happiness.

The Happiness Formula

If you thought happiness could be boiled down to just a few chemicals, think again! The science of happiness is like the ultimate recipe – a dash of genetics, a sprinkle of life circumstances, and many personal choices. As previously discussed, psychologists have found that about 50% of your happiness is due to genetics (thanks, Mom and Dad), 10% is influenced by your circumstances (like winning the lottery or losing your keys), and a whopping 40% is up to you!

Your daily habits, mindset, and actions play a huge role in how happy you feel. This has led to the booming field of Positive Psychology, where researchers like Martin Seligman study what makes life worth living. They've found that activities like practicing gratitude, nurturing relationships, and finding meaning can significantly boost your happiness levels.

Positive Psychology: Cultivating Well-being

Positive Psychology emerged in the late 20th century as a response to psychology's traditional focus on pathology and dysfunction. Rather than solely concentrating on treating mental illness, Positive Psychology aims to study and promote well-being, resilience, and human flourishing.

At the core of Positive Psychology lies the concept of subjective well-being (SWB), which encompasses three main components:

1. **Life Satisfaction:** This refers to a cognitive evaluation of one's life. It involves assessing whether one's life meets one's expectations and desires.
2. **Positive Affect:** Positive emotions such as joy, gratitude, and contentment contribute to overall happiness and well-being.
3. **Absence of Negative Affect:** Reducing negative emotions like sadness, anger, and anxiety also plays a crucial role in determining happiness.

Positive Psychology emphasizes cultivating positive emotions, engaging in meaningful activities, fostering positive relationships, finding purpose and meaning in life, and developing resilience in the face of adversity. By focusing on strengths and virtues rather than weaknesses and deficits, Positive Psychology offers practical strategies for enhancing happiness and well-being.

The Neurobiology of Happiness: Insights from Brain Science

Neurobiological (it took me 3 times to even pronounce this right) research has provided fascinating insights into the neural basis of happiness, revealing the complex interplay of neurotransmitters, neural circuits, and brain structures involved in emotional regulation and well-being.

1. **Neurotransmitters:** Neurotransmitters are chemical messengers that play critical roles in regulating mood and emotions. Key players include:
- *Serotonin*, often called the "feel-good" chemical, is associated with feelings of happiness, contentment, and well-being.
- *Dopamine* is involved in reward processing and motivation, contributing to feelings of pleasure and satisfaction.
- *Endorphins*, sometimes called the body's natural painkillers, are released during activities like exercise and laughter, producing feelings of euphoria and happiness.

2. **Prefrontal Cortex:** This region at the front of out brain, particularly the left prefrontal cortex, is associated with positive emotions and well-being. When active, it is linked to feelings of happiness, optimism, and resilience.

3. **Limbic System:** The limbic system, including structures such as the amygdala and hippocampus, plays a crucial role in processing emotions and emotional memories. Dysfunction in these brain regions has been linked to mood disorders such as depression and anxiety.

4. **Neuroplasticity:** The brain exhibits remarkable plasticity, meaning it can change and adapt in response to experiences and environmental influences. Practices like mindfulness, meditation, and cognitive-behavioral therapy (CBT) have been shown to promote neuroplasticity and positive brain changes associated with increased happiness and well-being.

Understanding how our brain creates and maintains happiness provides valuable insights into the mechanisms responsible for our emotional well-being. This knowledge opens up potential avenues for interventions and therapies aimed at enhancing happiness and mitigating psychological distress.

A Prescription for Joy

In summary, Positive Psychology and the neurobiology of happiness offer complementary perspectives on understanding and promoting well-being. By combining insights from psychological research with advances in neuroscience, we can better understand what it means to live a fulfilling and happy life and develop evidence-based strategies for enhancing happiness and resilience in ourselves and others.

What have we learned from this joyous journey through the science of happiness? Well, happiness isn't just about chasing thrills or avoiding bad vibes. It's about understanding the delightful dance of brain chemicals, embracing a positive mindset, and connecting with others. And remember, sometimes the best way to find happiness is to stop searching so hard for it and enjoy the little moments – like reading a humorously scientific article on happiness.

In the end, happiness is both an art and a science, like trying to mix baking soda and vinegar without making a mess. But hey, if all else fails, laugh – it's scientifically proven to make you feel better.

Reflection Questions

What makes you happy at work?

How do happiness and productivity influence each other?

CHAPTER 4

CREATING A POSITIVE WORK ENVIRONMENT OR CIRCUS

In the grand circus of life, there's a unique ring reserved for the workplace. And just like any good circus, the ringmaster–your fearless leader–can turn it from a dull, dreary place into a spectacle of positivity and productivity.

In today's fast-paced and competitive business landscape, fostering a positive work environment is essential for the success and sustainability of any organization. A positive work environment not only enhances employee morale and satisfaction but also leads to increased productivity, innovation, and overall organizational performance. This chapter will explore various strategies and best practices for creating and maintaining a positive work environment.

Understanding the Importance of a Positive Work Environment

A positive work environment is characterized by factors such as trust, respect, open communication, collaboration, recognition, and a sense of belonging among employees. Research has consistently shown that organizations with a positive workplace culture experience higher employee engagement, lower turnover rates, and better financial results. Moreover, a positive work environment fosters creativity, problem-solving, and a willingness to take risks, which are essential for driving innovation and staying ahead in today's dynamic business environment.

Critical Elements of a Positive Work Environment

1. **Leadership and Management:** Effective leadership plays a crucial role in shaping the culture and climate of an organization. In every circus, the ringmaster stands out with their dazzling costume and commanding presence. Leaders, too, need to lead by example. If you want your team to be punctual, don't stroll in at noon with a latte and a yoga mat. If you value work-life balance, don't send emails at 3 AM. Imagine the boss dressed in a sequined suit, twirling a baton and proclaiming, "Behold, I am the epitome of punctuality and balance!" It's a memorable (and hilarious) way to set the right example.

2. **Open Communication:** Good communication is the center ring of any successful workplace circus. Leaders should be like charismatic ringmasters, guiding the show with clarity and enthusiasm. Hold regular "circus meetings" where everyone can share their ideas while juggling (metaphorically, unless you're a really talented team). Encourage open dialogue with a fun twist, like a "clown horn" that anyone can honk when speaking up. It sounds silly, but it ensures everyone feels heard and valued. Open communication is essential for building trust and fostering collaboration within the organization. Employees should feel comfortable expressing their ideas, opinions, and feedback without fear of judgment or reprisal. Regular communication channels, such as team meetings, one-on-one sessions, and feedback mechanisms, should be established to facilitate dialogue and exchange of information.

3. **Employee Recognition and Appreciation:** Every circus has its magicians, and in the workplace, appreciation is the magic spell that makes everything better. A simple "thank you" can transform an ordinary workday into a celebration. But why stop there? Hand out "Best Email Sent Today" awards or "Most Enthusiastic Coffee Drinker" trophies. These small acts of recognition can make employees feel valued and motivated. And who doesn't like a bit of magical flair at the office? Recognizing and appreciating employees' contributions and achievements is vital for boosting morale and motivation. This can take various forms, including verbal praise, written commendations, awards, bonuses, or promotion opportunities. Genuine recognition fosters a sense of pride and loyalty among employees, encouraging them to go above and beyond in their roles. Leaders should regularly recognize and acknowledge the contributions and achievements of their employees. Whether through verbal praise, written commendations, or rewards and incentives, rec-

ognition fosters a sense of appreciation and validation, boosting morale and happiness.

4. **Work-Life Balance:** Maintaining work-life balance is like swinging on a trapeze—daring, thrilling, and requiring precise timing. Leaders should encourage their team to take breaks and prioritize personal time, even if it means scheduling "mandatory nap times" during the day. Picture your boss in a onesie, ringing a bell and announcing, "Nap time, everyone!" It sounds absurd, but it proves that rest is essential for productivity. Plus, who wouldn't want to see their boss in a onesie? Supporting employees' work-life balance is critical for promoting overall well-being and reducing stress and burnout. Organizations can offer flexible work arrangements, such as telecommuting, flexible hours, and paid time off, to accommodate employees' personal and professional commitments. Encouraging employees to take regular breaks and vacations and participate in wellness initiatives also contributes to a healthier and more productive workforce.

5. **Continuous Learning and Development:** Investing in employee learning and development not only enhances individual skills and competencies but also demonstrates a commitment to their growth and career advancement. Providing access to training programs, workshops, mentorship opportunities, and tuition reimbursement encourages employees to expand their knowledge and stay relevant in their respective fields.

6. **Diversity and Inclusion:** What circus would be enticing if they only had the ringmaster and only dancing bears? Embracing diversity and inclusion is critical for creating a welcoming and inclusive work environment where all employees feel valued, respected, and empowered to contribute their unique perspectives and talents. Organizations should foster a culture of equity and fairness, promote diversity in recruitment and hiring

practices, and provide equal opportunities for advancement regardless of gender, race, ethnicity, or background.
7. **Transparency:** Let's face it: transparency in leadership is like juggling. It's all about keeping multiple balls in the air—clarity, honesty, and open communication—without dropping any and causing chaos. Imagine your boss trying to juggle these balls while riding a unicycle. Hilarious, right? Yet, when done right, it prevents misunderstandings and builds trust. So, dear leaders, be transparent, even if it feels like you're balancing on a tightrope without a net.
8. **An Environment of Innovation:** Innovation is the high-flying trapeze act that keeps the workplace exciting. Encourage your team to take risks and think outside the box. Hold brainstorming sessions in a "Big Top" tent (or just a conference room with circus music playing). Reward the craziest ideas with the "Flying Elephant" awards because sometimes the most outlandish ideas lead to the most significant innovations. And remember, even if an idea crashes and burns, at least you'll have a good laugh and a valuable lesson.
9. **Delegation:** Delegation is a tightrope act that requires balance and trust. Leaders who micromanage are like tightrope walkers who keep looking down—terrified and bound to fall. Trust your team, hand over the reins, and watch them perform amazing feats. And if they stumble, be there with a safety net (and maybe a trampoline for extra bounce). After all, even the most fantastic acrobats had a few tumbles before mastering their craft.

Implementing Strategies for Creating a Positive Work Environment

1. **Conducting Employee Surveys:** Regularly soliciting employee feedback through surveys or focus groups can provide valuable

insights into their perceptions, needs, and concerns regarding the work environment. Organizations can use this feedback to identify areas for improvement and implement targeted initiatives to address issues and enhance employee satisfaction.

2. **Promoting Team-Building Activities:** Organizing team-building activities, such as retreats, workshops, or social events, can strengthen relationships among team members, improve communication, and foster a sense of camaraderie and collaboration. These activities provide opportunities for employees to interact outside of their usual work context and develop a sense of belonging to the team and organization.

3. **Creating a Positive Physical Workspace:** The physical environment significantly shapes the overall employee experience. Organizations should design workspaces that are comfortable, ergonomic, and conducive to productivity and creativity. Providing amenities such as relaxation areas, healthy snacks, and natural light can contribute to employee well-being and satisfaction.

4. **Empowering Employees:** Empowering employees to make decisions and take ownership of their work fosters a sense of autonomy, responsibility, and accountability. Organizations should encourage employees to voice their ideas, initiate projects, and participate in decision-making processes. Empowerment creates a sense of ownership and pride in one's work, leading to greater job satisfaction and engagement.

5. **Leading by Example:** Leaders and managers play a critical role in setting the tone for the organizational culture. They should exemplify the values of respect, integrity, and positivity in their interactions with employees and stakeholders. Leaders can inspire trust, loyalty, and commitment among their teams by demonstrating empathy, humility, and a willingness to listen.

Leadership and Culture

The Role of Leadership in Fostering a Happiness Culture

Leadership plays a pivotal role in fostering happiness within an organization. Leaders have the power to shape the culture, values, and climate of the workplace, directly influencing the level of happiness and satisfaction among employees. Here are several key ways in which leadership contributes to fostering happiness:

Setting the Tone: Leaders set the tone for the organization through their actions, behaviors, and attitudes. When leaders demonstrate positivity, optimism, and enthusiasm, they create a ripple effect that influences the overall mood and morale of the workplace. Leaders inspire employees to adopt a similar mindset and outlook by modeling happiness and well-being.

Creating a Positive Work Environment: Leaders are responsible for creating and maintaining a positive work environment where employees feel valued, respected, and appreciated. This involves promoting open communication, trust, collaboration, and recognition. Leaders should foster a culture of inclusivity, where diverse perspectives are welcomed and celebrated, contributing to employees' sense of belonging and happiness.

Supporting Employee Well-Being: Leaders play a crucial role in supporting the well-being of their employees. This includes providing resources and initiatives to promote work-life balance, such as flexible work arrangements, wellness programs, and mental health support. Leaders should prioritize employee health and happiness, recognizing that a healthy workforce is essential for organizational success.

Empowering and Engaging Employees: Effective leaders empower and engage their employees by involving them in decision-making processes, providing autonomy and opportunities for growth and development. When employees feel trusted, valued, and empowered to contribute their ideas and talents, they experience a greater sense of fulfillment and happiness in their roles.

Offering Feedback and Appreciation: Providing constructive feedback and support helps employees grow and improve, contributing to overall job satisfaction and happiness. A positive culture recognizes and appreciates employees' contributions and achievements. When employees feel acknowledged and rewarded for their efforts, they experience a boost in morale and motivation, leading to greater happiness and job satisfaction.

Leading with Empathy and Compassion: Empathetic leadership is essential for fostering happiness and well-being in the workplace. Leaders should demonstrate empathy, understanding, and compassion towards their employees, recognizing their individual needs, challenges, and aspirations. Leaders build trust, loyalty, and a supportive work environment conducive to happiness and success by showing genuine care and concern for their team members.

Building a Positive Organizational Culture

Building a positive organizational culture is crucial for fostering happiness among employees for several reasons:

Sense of Belonging: A positive organizational culture creates a sense of belonging among employees, making them feel like valued members of a community. When individuals feel connected to their organization and colleagues, they experience greater satisfaction and happiness in their work.

Increased Engagement: A positive culture promotes employee engagement by aligning values, goals, and behaviors. Engaged employees are more invested in their work, leading to higher motivation, productivity, and happiness.

Enhanced Well-being: A positive culture prioritizes employee well-being by supporting work-life balance, providing resources for stress management, and fostering a supportive environment. Employees who feel cared for and supported by their organization are happier and more satisfied with their jobs.

Open Communication: A positive culture encourages open communication and transparency, allowing employees to freely voice their opinions, ideas, and concerns. When employees feel heard and valued, they experience greater trust and satisfaction, contributing to their overall happiness.

Opportunities for Growth: A positive culture emphasizes learning and development, allowing employees to grow, advance, and reach their full potential. When individuals are encouraged to develop their skills and pursue their career goals, they experience a sense of fulfillment and happiness in their work.

Emotional Intelligence and Empathy: A positive culture is characterized by leaders and colleagues demonstrating emotional intelligence and empathy. Leaders who understand and respond to their employees' emotions and needs create a supportive and compassionate work environment conducive to happiness and well-being.

Alignment with Values: A positive culture is aligned with the organization's values, mission, and vision, providing employees with a sense of purpose and meaning in their work. When individuals feel their work contributes to something meaningful and worthwhile, they experience greater fulfillment and happiness.

Creating and maintaining a positive work environment is a continuous process that requires commitment, effort, and collaboration from all levels of the organization. By prioritizing factors such as leadership, communication, recognition, work-life balance, learning, diversity, and inclusion, organizations can cultivate a culture where employees feel valued, motivated, and empowered to perform at their best. Investing in a positive work environment not only benefits employees' well-being and satisfaction but also contributes to organizational success and competitiveness in the long run.

Leadership plays a critical role in fostering happiness within an organization by setting the tone, creating a positive work environment, supporting employee well-being, empowering and engaging employees, offering recognition and feedback, and leading with empathy and compassion. When leaders prioritize happiness and well-being, they create a culture where employees thrive, leading to increased motivation, productivity, and organizational success.

Building a positive organizational culture is essential for fostering happiness among employees by promoting a sense of belonging, increasing engagement, enhancing well-being, encouraging open communication, providing growth opportunities, offering recognition and appreciation, demonstrating emotional intelligence and empathy, and aligning with values. Organizations that prioritize a positive culture create environments where employees thrive, leading to increased satisfaction, productivity, and success.

In the end, creating a positive work environment is all about balance, humor, and a bit of showmanship. Leaders who embrace their inner ringmaster can turn the workplace into a vibrant, engaging circus where everyone is excited to perform. So, step right up, ladies and gentlemen, and witness the most incredible show on earth—a workplace where positivity, productivity, and plenty of laughs are always center stage.

Reflection Questions

How do you, as a leader, impact the happiness of your workplace?

What methods or strategies have you implemented to foster a happy workplace?

CHAPTER 5

NURTURING EMPLOYEE ENGAGEMENT AND SATISFACTION

In the dynamic landscape of modern workplaces, employee engagement and satisfaction are pivotal pillars for organizational success. As companies strive to cultivate environments where employees feel valued, motivated, and connected to their work, the significance of fostering engagement and satisfaction cannot be overstated. This chapter explores the intricacies of these concepts and offers actionable insights for nurturing them within any organizational framework.

Understanding Employee Engagement and Satisfaction

Employee engagement encompasses employees' emotional commitment toward their organization and its goals. It transcends job satisfaction and delves into passion, enthusiasm, and dedication. Engaged employees are deeply invested in their work, resulting in higher productivity, more significant innovation, and enhanced customer satisfaction.

On the other hand, employee satisfaction pertains to the contentment and fulfillment individuals derive from their roles, compensation, working conditions, and organizational culture. While satisfaction alone may not guarantee engagement, it is a foundational element upon which engagement can thrive.

The Importance of Employee Engagement and Satisfaction

Organizations that prioritize employee engagement and satisfaction reap a myriad of benefits. Engaged employees are likelier to go the extra mile, contributing innovative ideas and solutions. They exhibit higher levels of commitment and are less likely to seek opportunities elsewhere, reducing turnover rates and associated costs. Moreover, engaged employees are brand ambassadors, positively influencing customer perceptions and loyalty.

Strategies for Nurturing Engagement and Satisfaction

1. Foster a Positive Work Environment

Cultivate a culture of trust, respect, and open communication. Encourage collaboration and provide opportunities for employees to voice their opinions and concerns. Creating a positive work environment is crucial for the success and sustainability of any organization. It is the soil in which productivity, innovation, and collaboration grow. Fostering a positive work environment is an ongoing process that adapts as the organization evolves. It requires commitment from all levels of the organization, particularly from top leadership. By implementing these strategies, organizations can create environments that boost performance and ensure that employees are engaged, satisfied, and aligned with the organization's goals. In this nurturing setting, the organization and its people can thrive together.

Understanding the Positive Work Environment
A positive work environment is characterized by a supportive atmosphere that promotes employee well-being, productivity, and mutual respect among colleagues and supervisors. It involves more than just physical surroundings; it encompasses the cultural and emotional layers of the workplace. This environment nurtures employees' abilities to perform their duties effectively while feeling valued and respected.

Critical Elements of a Positive Work Environment

- **Communication:** Clear, transparent, and open communication is the backbone of a positive work environment. It ensures that employees are well-informed, engaged, and comfortable sharing their ideas and concerns.

- **Respect:** Mutual respect among all employees, regardless of their position, fosters a sense of dignity and equality. This includes respecting personal boundaries, valuing diverse perspectives, and promoting inclusivity.
- **Recognition:** Acknowledging employees' efforts and achievements boosts morale and motivates them to maintain high performance. Recognition should be timely, fair, and linked to specific accomplishments or behaviors.
- **Trust:** Cultivating trust involves consistency, reliability, and integrity in interactions and decisions. Trust leads to greater autonomy, reduced conflicts, and a supportive atmosphere where employees feel secure taking risks and innovating.
- **Work-Life Balance/Blend:** Encouraging a managed blend between professional and personal life helps prevent burnout and supports overall employee health. Flexible working hours, remote work options, and understanding personal commitments are ways to support work-life blend. We emphasize that blending is more realistic to balance due to the continuous merger between personal and professional lives.

Strategies to Foster a Positive Work Environment

1. **Develop Strong Leadership:** Leaders set the tone for the workplace environment. Influential leaders inspire, guide, and support their teams. They practice empathy, are approachable, and promote the well-being of their staff.
2. **Build Team Cohesion:** Regular team-building activities and social events can strengthen employee relationships. This can range from simple lunch outings to more structured team development exercises.

3. **Create a Safe and Healthy Workplace:** Ensure the physical workplace is safe, clean, and pleasant. Consider ergonomics, adequate lighting, ventilation, and quiet spaces for rest and recovery.
4. **Encourage Professional Development:** Offer opportunities for employees to enhance their skills and advance their careers within the organization. This shows investment in their professional growth and personal achievements.
5. **Implement Fair Policies:** Develop and enforce policies that promote fairness and equality. Clear guidelines on conduct, performance expectations, and dispute resolution procedures contribute to a just workplace.
6. **Promote Transparency:** Regular updates about the organization's status and changes help employees feel valued and included. Transparency in decision-making processes also enhances trust.
7. **Support Innovation and Feedback:** Encourage employees to contribute ideas and improvements and create mechanisms to capture this feedback. Innovations should be celebrated, and constructive feedback should be acted upon.

Measuring the Impact

To gauge the effectiveness of efforts to foster a positive work environment, leaders can use employee satisfaction surveys, turnover rates, productivity metrics, and feedback during performance reviews. Additionally, direct observation and informal conversations can provide insights into the workplace's health.

2. Promote Work-Life Balance/Blend

Recognize the importance of employee well-being by offering flexible work arrangements, wellness programs, and adequate time off. Balance fosters rejuvenation and prevents burnout, leading to higher job satisfaction. In today's fast-paced world, achieving a healthy balance between work and personal life has become increasingly challenging. However, it is essential for employees' well-being and productivity and organizations' long-term success.

Promoting work-life balance is not only beneficial for employees' well-being but also for the success and sustainability of organizations. Employers can create environments where employees feel supported, valued, and empowered to achieve balance in their professional and personal lives. Fostering work-life balance fosters happier, healthier, and more engaged employees who contribute to the organization's success.

Understanding Work-Life Balance/Blend

Work-life balance refers to the equilibrium individuals seek between their professional responsibilities and personal pursuits, such as family, hobbies, and self-care. It involves managing time and energy effectively to meet work-related demands and individual needs. Achieving work-life balance is not about equal time allocation but rather about finding harmony and fulfillment in both domains.

The Importance of Work-Life Balance/Blend

- **Employee Well-being:** Balancing work and personal life reduces stress, anxiety, and burnout, promoting overall well-being and mental health. It allows individuals to recharge, relax, and engage in activities that bring them joy and fulfillment.
- **Increased Productivity:** Research has shown that employees with a healthy work-life balance are more productive, creative, and focused during working hours. They can better manage their time, prioritize tasks, and maintain high performance levels.

- **Retention and Recruitment:** Organizations that prioritize work-life balance attract and retain top talent. Employees are more likely to stay with employers who value their well-being and offer flexibility to accommodate their personal lives.
- **Enhanced Engagement:** When employees feel supported in balancing their work and personal responsibilities, they are more engaged, committed, and loyal to their organization. They are also more likely to go above and beyond in their roles.

Strategies for Promoting Work-Life Balance/Blend

1. **Flexible Work Arrangements:** Offer flexible scheduling options, such as remote work, flextime, compressed workweeks, or job sharing. Allow employees to tailor their work hours to accommodate personal commitments and preferences.
2. **Set Clear Boundaries:** Encourage employees to establish clear boundaries between work and personal life. Respect non-working hours and avoid sending emails or assigning tasks outside designated work times.
3. **Promote Time Management Skills:** Provide training and resources to help employees improve their time management and prioritization skills. Encourage them to set realistic goals, delegate tasks when necessary, and avoid overcommitting.
4. **Encourage Regular Breaks:** Emphasize the importance of taking regular breaks throughout the workday to rest and recharge. Encourage employees to step away from their desks, go for walks, or engage in activities that help them relax and refocus.
5. **Lead by Example:** Leaders play a crucial role in promoting work-life balance by modeling healthy behaviors and prioritizing their well-being. Encourage leaders to take vacations, use their allotted time off, and maintain boundaries between work and personal life.

6. **Provide Supportive Policies and Benefits:** Offer benefits such as paid time off, parental leave, childcare assistance, and flexible spending accounts to support employees' personal needs. Review and update policies regularly to ensure they align with employees' evolving needs.
7. **Promote a Culture of Respect and Understanding**: Foster a culture where employees feel comfortable discussing their obligations and seeking support when needed. Encourage open communication and empathy among team members.

Measuring Work-Life Balance
The organization's work-life balance can be assessed through surveys, focus groups, and interviews to gather employee feedback. Additionally, monitoring metrics such as absenteeism, turnover rates, and productivity levels can provide insights into the effectiveness of work-life balance initiatives.

3. Invest in Professional Development

Empower employees to grow and develop by offering training programs, mentorship opportunities, and career advancement pathways. Investing in employees' professional growth demonstrates a commitment to their success and fosters loyalty.

Professional development is critical to employee engagement, satisfaction, and overall organizational success. It involves providing opportunities for employees to enhance their skills, knowledge, and competencies, enabling them to excel in their current roles and prepare for future challenges.

Investing in professional development is essential for nurturing a knowledgeable, skilled, and motivated workforce. By committing to the growth and development of its employees, an organization not only enhances its operational capabilities but also builds a resilient and adaptable workforce equipped to handle future challenges.

Understanding Professional Development

Professional development encompasses a wide range of activities designed to enhance an employee's capabilities and career prospects. These activities can include training workshops, seminars, conferences, mentoring programs, and higher education opportunities. The goal is to foster a lifelong learning culture that motivates employees to grow professionally and personally.

The Importance of Professional Development

- **Enhanced Employee Performance:** Well-trained employees perform their duties more efficiently and with greater confidence. Professional development helps bridge gaps in knowledge and skills, leading to better job performance.
- **Increased Employee Engagement:** Employees who see investment in their growth are more likely to feel valued and connected to the company. This increases their engagement levels and commitment to the organization.
- **Attraction and Retention of Talent:** Organizations that offer comprehensive professional development opportunities are more attractive to potential employees and more likely to retain their current workforce.
- **Cultivation of Future Leaders:** Professional development programs are crucial for preparing the next generation of leaders. These programs allow companies to develop their talent in-house, ensuring a continuous flow of qualified individuals ready to step into leadership roles.
- **Adaptability to Industry Changes:** Continuous learning and development help organizations stay competitive in rapidly changing industries by ensuring that their employees are up-to-date with the latest technologies, methodologies, and best practices.

Strategies for Promoting Professional Development

1. **Assess Training Needs:** Regularly assess employees' training and development needs through surveys, interviews, and performance evaluations. This assessment should align with the organization's strategic goals and the specific competencies required for each role.
2. **Offer Diverse Training Methods:** Provide various training methods to cater to different learning styles and needs. This could include online courses, in-person workshops, webinars, on-the-job training, and peer learning opportunities.
3. **Support Career Advancement:** Create clear career paths within the organization and support employees in pursuing these paths. This can include succession planning and providing opportunities for employees to take on new challenges or leadership roles.
4. **Encourage Mentorship:** Establish a mentorship program where experienced employees can guide less experienced ones. This not only aids in skill transfer but also helps build strong professional relationships and enhance team cohesion.
5. **Allocate Resources Effectively:** Dedicate a budget for professional development and ensure it is used effectively. Consider the return on investment for training programs and prioritize spending on those with the highest impact.
6. **Recognize and Reward Development:** Acknowledge employees who make significant efforts in their professional development. This recognition can be through certificates, awards, or even promotions.
7. **Evaluate and Iterate:** Regularly evaluate the effectiveness of professional development programs. Use employee feedback to make necessary adjustments and improvements to the training offerings.

Implementing Professional Development Programs

To effectively implement a professional development program, organizations should:

- **Plan**: Define clear objectives and outcomes for each training initiative.
- **Execute**: Deliver training using appropriate formats and resources.
- **Review**: Continuously assess the program's effectiveness in meeting its objectives and make adjustments as necessary.

4. Recognize and Reward Performance

Acknowledge and celebrate individual and team achievements. Implement reward systems that align with organizational values and goals, motivating employees to excel and reinforcing desired behaviors.

Recognizing and rewarding employee performance is a critical aspect of talent management that directly impacts organizational success. Effective recognition and reward programs not only motivate employees but also foster a culture of appreciation and performance excellence.

Recognizing and rewarding performance is crucial in motivating employees, enhancing their engagement, and driving organizational success. An effective recognition and reward program should be well-planned, inclusive, and aligned with the company's strategic goals.

Understanding the Value of Recognition and Reward

Recognition and reward programs are designed to acknowledge employee achievements, reinforce behaviors aligned with business goals, and increase employee engagement and loyalty. When employees feel that their hard work is recognized and rewarded, they are more likely to be productive, satisfied, and committed to their employer.

Principles of Effective Recognition

- **Timeliness:** Recognition should be given as close to the event or achievement as possible to reinforce desired behaviors and enhance their impact.
- **Relevance:** Rewards and recognition should be aligned with the achievements they are meant to acknowledge. This ensures that the reward is seen as appropriate and meaningful.
- **Consistency:** Applying recognition consistently across the organization avoids perceptions of favoritism and ensures fairness.
- **Personalization:** Tailoring recognition to fit each employee's individual preferences and motivations can enhance the reward's personal value and emotional impact.

Types of Rewards

1. **Monetary Rewards:** Includes bonuses, raises, profit sharing, and stock options. These rewards are straightforward and highly valued by employees but can be costly for the organization.
2. **Non-Monetary Rewards:** Includes public recognition, certificates, plaques, and thank-you notes. These are cost-effective and can be very effective in building a positive workplace culture.
3. **Experiential Rewards:** Involves providing experiences, such as trips, dinners, or tickets to events. These create lasting memories and can be highly motivating.
4. **Development Opportunities:** Offering opportunities for professional growth, such as training, conferences, or mentoring, rewards employees while also benefiting the organization by enhancing their skills.
5. **Work-life balance Enhancements:** These include flexible working hours, additional vacation time, or remote work opportunities. These rewards recognize the employee's effort by contributing to their quality of life outside work.

Strategies for Rewarding and Recognizing Employees

1. **Set Clear Criteria:** Define clear and objective criteria for what constitutes rewardable performance. This helps employees understand what is expected of them and how they can achieve recognition.
2. **Diverse Recognition Programs:** Implement a variety of recognition programs to address the different ways people prefer to be recognized. This could include peer-to-peer recognition, formal awards ceremonies, or spontaneous verbal recognition from leadership.
3. **Involve Leadership:** Active participation by leaders in recognition programs lends importance to the initiatives and can significantly boost morale.
4. **Regular Feedback:** Combine formal rewards with regular, constructive feedback so employees know how they perform and what they can improve.
5. **Utilize Technology:** Consider using software platforms that facilitate recognition, such as social feeds where employees can publicly praise their colleagues. These platforms also keep records of accomplishments.
6. **Evaluate and Adjust:** Regularly review the effectiveness of recognition programs. Solicit employee feedback to understand what works and what doesn't and adjust programs accordingly to maintain their effectiveness and relevance.

Implementing a Recognition and Reward Program

To effectively implement a recognition and reward program, organizations should plan strategically:

- **Engage Stakeholders**: Include input from across the organization to ensure the program meets all employees' diverse needs and expectations.

- **Communicate Clearly:** Ensure that all employees understand how the program works and how they can participate in or benefit from it.
- **Monitor and Measure:** Set metrics to assess the program's impact on employee engagement, satisfaction, and performance, and use this data to refine the program over time.

5. Provide Meaningful Work

Connect employees' roles to the broader purpose and goals of the organization. Help them understand how their contributions make a difference, instilling a sense of pride and fulfillment in their work.

The quest for meaning and purpose in work is a fundamental human need. Employees who find their work meaningful are more engaged, satisfied, and committed to their organizations.

Providing meaningful work is essential for fostering employee engagement, satisfaction, and well-being. By aligning work with organizational mission and values, providing opportunities for growth and development, and fostering a culture of purpose and meaning, organizations can create environments where employees thrive and feel fulfilled in their work. Investing in meaningful work benefits individual employees and contributes to the organization's long-term success and sustainability.

Understanding Meaningful Work

Meaningful work goes beyond the completion of tasks and the pursuit of financial rewards. It involves a deep sense of fulfillment, purpose, and alignment with one's values and aspirations. While meaningful work is subjective and varies from person to person, it often involves positively impacting others, contributing to a greater cause, or experiencing personal growth and development.

The Importance of Meaningful Work

- **Employee Engagement:** Employees who find their work meaningful are more engaged and committed to their organizations. They are willing to invest extra effort and take on additional responsibilities to contribute to the organization's success.
- **Job Satisfaction:** Meaningful work is a significant driver of job satisfaction. Employees who derive meaning from their work are likelier to experience higher levels of fulfillment, happiness, and overall well-being.
- **Retention and Recruitment:** Organizations that provide meaningful work attract and retain top talent. Employees are more likely to stay with employers who offer opportunities for personal and professional growth and allow them to make a difference in the world.
- **Performance and Productivity:** Employees who find their work meaningful are more motivated, focused, and productive. They are driven by intrinsic factors such as passion and purpose, leading to higher levels of performance and innovation.

What Makes Work Meaningful?

1. **Contribution to a Greater Purpose:** Meaningful work often involves making a positive impact on others, whether it's helping customers achieve their goals, improving society, or advancing a noble cause. All players want to contribute to the team's success.
2. **Personal Growth and Development:** Meaningful work provides opportunities for learning, growth, and mastery. Employees feel fulfilled when challenged, develop new skills, and achieve personal and professional milestones.
3. **Autonomy and Empowerment:** Meaningful work gives employees a sense of autonomy and control over their tasks and deci-

sions. They feel empowered to make meaningful contributions and take ownership of their work.

4. **Recognition and Appreciation:** Feeling valued and appreciated for their contributions enhances employees' sense of meaning and purpose. Recognition can come from peers, leaders, or customers and can take various forms, such as praise, rewards, or promotions.

Strategies for Providing Meaningful Work

1. **Align Work with Organizational Mission and Values:** Ensure employees understand how their work contributes to the organization's mission and goals. Help them see the bigger picture and how their efforts make a difference.
2. **Provide Opportunities for Growth and Development:** Offer training, mentorship, and career advancement opportunities to support employees' personal and professional growth. Encourage them to set challenging goals and pursue their passions.
3. **Foster a Culture of Purpose and Meaning:** Create a workplace culture that values and celebrates meaningful work. Encourage open communication, collaboration, and teamwork, and recognize and reward employees who exemplify the organization's values.
4. **Promote Work-Life Integration:** Support employees in achieving a balance between their work and personal lives by offering flexible work arrangements, promoting well-being initiatives, and encouraging employees to pursue their interests outside of work.
5. **Empower Employees to Make a Difference:** Give employees autonomy and decision-making authority over their work. Encourage them to take initiative, explore new ideas, and make a positive impact in their roles and beyond.

6. Encourage Feedback and Continuous Improvement

Establish channels for feedback and actively solicit input from employees at all levels. Use feedback to identify areas for improvement and implement changes that enhance the employee experience.

In today's fast-paced and ever-evolving business environment, adapting and continuously improving is crucial for maintaining competitive advantage. Feedback is a vital component of this process, serving as a bridge that connects individual and organizational growth.

Creating a culture that embraces feedback and continuous improvement is essential for any organization aiming to stay relevant and competitive. Organizations can foster an environment where constant learning and adaptation become the norm by encouraging open communication, training employees on effective feedback mechanisms, and aligning improvement initiatives with strategic goals. This environment drives business success and enhances employee satisfaction and engagement, creating a virtuous cycle of growth and development.

The Importance of Feedback and Continuous Improvement
Feedback and continuous improvement are interconnected concepts that drive business success and employee satisfaction. Feedback provides the insights necessary for identifying areas of improvement, while constant improvement focuses on implementing changes that enhance performance, processes, and products.

- **Enhanced Performance**: Regular feedback helps individuals and teams understand their strengths and weaknesses, leading to better performance.
- **Increased Agility:** Organizations that prioritize continuous improvement are better equipped to respond to changes in the market and technological advancements.

- **Employee Engagement:** Employees who feel their contributions are recognized and their suggestions for improvements are taken seriously are more engaged and committed.
- **Innovation:** A culture that encourages feedback and continuous improvement is inherently conducive to innovation, as new ideas are valued and explored.

Building a Feedback-Rich Environment

1. **Promote Open Communication:** Foster an environment where open and honest communication is encouraged and valued. Ensure that employees at all levels feel safe to express their thoughts and feedback without fear of negative repercussions.
2. **Train on Feedback Delivery and Reception:** Provide training to both managers and employees on how to give and receive feedback effectively. Emphasize the importance of constructive feedback and teach skills that facilitate respectful and productive feedback sessions.
3. **Regular Check-Ins:** Implement regular one-on-one meetings between employees and managers to discuss progress, challenges, and feedback. This regular interaction helps build trust and ensures timely and relevant feedback.
4. **360-Degree Feedback:** Utilize 360-degree feedback systems that allow employees to receive insights from peers, subordinates, and supervisors. This comprehensive view helps individuals understand how their actions affect others in the organization.

Cultivating a Culture of Continuous Improvement

1. **Set Clear Expectations:** Communicate that continuous improvement is a valued part of the organizational culture. Set expectations that all team members should regularly look for ways to enhance their work processes and outputs.

2. **Empower Employees:** Empower employees by giving them the tools and authority to make minor improvements in their work without needing to go through excessive bureaucratic procedures.
3. **Reward and Recognize Improvements:** Establish a system to reward and recognize contributions to process improvements, efficiency gains, or innovative ideas. Recognition can be as simple as public acknowledgment or as significant as financial incentives.
4. **Incorporate Improvement into Strategic Goals:** Align continuous improvement initiatives with strategic organizational goals. Show how these efforts contribute to the company's broader objectives to reinforce their importance.

Implementing Effective Feedback and Continuous Improvement Processes

1. **Feedback Mechanisms:** Implement feedback mechanisms such as suggestion boxes, digital forums, and regular surveys. Make it straightforward for employees to provide feedback at any time.
2. **Action on Feedback:** Ensure feedback does not go unnoticed. Act on the feedback received and communicate what changes are being made. This action reinforces the value of sharing feedback.
3. **Continuous Learning Opportunities:** Provide employees with opportunities to learn and develop new skills to contribute to continuous improvement efforts. This could include workshops, seminars, and access to courses.
4. **Review and Iterate:** Regularly review the effectiveness of the feedback and continuous improvement processes. Be open to making changes in the approach as necessary to suit organizational needs and employee expectations better.

7. Lead by Example

Leadership plays a pivotal role in shaping organizational culture and employee engagement. Lead with integrity, empathy, and authenticity, inspiring trust and confidence among team members.

Leadership is not merely about holding a position of authority; it's about inspiring, guiding, and empowering others to achieve their full potential. Leading by example is one of the most potent ways to influence others.

Leading by example is not just a leadership technique; it's a philosophy that embodies the essence of effective leadership. By demonstrating integrity, accountability, empathy, and a commitment to excellence, leaders can inspire and motivate their teams to reach new heights of success. Doing so creates a culture of trust, respect, and collaboration that propels the organization forward. As a leader, your actions speak louder than words—lead by example, and others will follow.

Understanding Leading by Example

Leading by example is the practice of embodying the values, behaviors, and principles that one expects from others. It involves demonstrating integrity, accountability, and commitment in one's actions and decisions. By setting a positive example, leaders inspire trust, motivate their teams, and foster a culture of excellence and accountability.

The Impact of Leading by Example

- **Inspires Trust and Respect:** When leaders consistently demonstrate integrity, honesty, and transparency, they earn the trust and respect of their teams. This trust forms the foundation of strong relationships and effective teamwork.
- **Sets the Tone for Organizational Culture:** Leaders serve as role models whose behaviors and attitudes are emulated by others. By

leading by example, leaders shape the culture of the organization, influencing how employees interact, collaborate, and perform.
- **Drives Accountability and Performance:** When leaders hold themselves to high standards and take ownership of their responsibilities, it sets a precedent for accountability throughout the organization. Employees are more likely to take ownership of their work and strive for excellence when they see their leaders doing the same.
- **Promotes Collaboration and Teamwork:** Leaders who lead by example foster an environment of collaboration and teamwork where individuals are encouraged to support and uplift one another. This creates a sense of camaraderie and unity among team members.

Strategies for Leading by Example

1. **Demonstrate Integrity:** Act with honesty, integrity, and consistency in all your interactions. Uphold ethical standards and be transparent about your decisions and actions.
2. **Communicate Effectively:** Practice active listening and communicate clearly, openly, and honestly with your team. Encourage feedback and be receptive to different perspectives.
3. **Take Initiative:** Be proactive and take the initiative to address challenges, solve problems, and pursue opportunities for improvement. Lead by example in demonstrating a growth mindset and resilience in the face of adversity.
4. **Empower and Develop Others:** Invest in your team members' growth and development. Provide mentorship, coaching, and opportunities for learning and skill development.
5. **Promote Work-Life Balance:** Prioritize your well-being and demonstrate the importance of work-life balance to your team. Encourage employees to take breaks, recharge, and prioritize self-care.

6. **Celebrate Successes and Learn from Failures:** Acknowledge and celebrate big and small achievements. Likewise, use setbacks and failures as learning opportunities, demonstrating resilience and a commitment to continuous improvement.
7. **Lead with Empathy and Compassion:** Show empathy and compassion towards your team members, understanding their needs, concerns, and challenges. Be supportive and approachable, fostering a culture of psychological safety and trust.

Implementing Leading by Example

1. **Self-Reflection:** Take time for self-reflection to assess your strengths, weaknesses, and areas for improvement. Continuously strive to grow and develop as a leader.
2. **Accountability:** Hold yourself accountable for your actions and decisions. Be willing to admit mistakes and take responsibility for addressing them.
3. **Feedback and Evaluation:** Seek feedback from your team members and peers on your leadership style and effectiveness. Use this feedback to identify areas for improvement and make necessary adjustments.
4. **Consistency:** Be consistent in your words and actions. Ensure that your behavior aligns with the values and expectations you set for your team.

Measuring Engagement and Satisfaction

Effective measurement is essential for gauging the impact of engagement and satisfaction initiatives and identifying areas for improvement. To gather insights into employee perceptions and experiences, utilize a combination of qualitative and quantitative methods, such as surveys, focus groups, and performance metrics. Regularly assess progress and adjust strategies accordingly to ensure continuous improvement.

Conclusion

Employee engagement and satisfaction are not merely buzzwords but fundamental drivers of organizational performance and success. By prioritizing employee well-being and engagement, organizations can create vibrant cultures where individuals thrive, driving innovation, productivity, and ultimately, sustainable growth. Embrace the journey of nurturing engagement and satisfaction, recognizing that investing in your employees yields dividends far beyond the bottom line.

Reflection Question

In what order would you prioritize the critical elements (Communication, Respect, Recognition, Trust, Work-Life Balance) of a Positive Workplace? And why?

CHAPTER 6

ENHANCING INDIVIDUAL HAPPINESS

Imagine waking up each morning with the energy of a caffeinated squirrel, ready to tackle the day with a smile plastered on your face. That, my friends, is the power of individual happiness. Not only does it make your life infinitely more enjoyable, but it also turns you into a beacon of joy, spreading cheer like confetti in a wind tunnel. Let's dive into why individual happiness is crucial to keep things light and giggle-worthy.

The Mood Domino Effect

Have you ever noticed how one grumpy person can ruin a perfectly good day faster than a cop pulling you over on your way to work? Happiness works the same way but in reverse. When you're happy, you radiate positive vibes like a human disco ball. Your happiness is infectious. It makes your coworkers smile and your friends laugh, and even that perpetually grumpy barista might give you an extra pump of caramel in your latte.

Productivity Boost (Or How to Turn into a Work Ninja)

It's a proven fact that happy people are productive people. It's science. Or maybe it's just common sense. Either way, you're more motivated, focused, and creative when you're happy. Imagine yourself as a work ninja, slicing through tasks with the precision of a samurai sword, all because you've got a grin on your face. Suddenly, even the most mundane tasks, like filling out spreadsheets, organizing the supply closet, or confronting customers feel like exciting adventures. Maybe not quite Lara Croft or Indiana Jones level, but close enough.

Health Benefits

Happiness isn't just good for your soul; it's fantastic for your body, too. It lowers stress, reduces the risk of heart disease, and even strengthens your immune system. So, in a way, being happy makes you a superhero. Sure, you might not have the ability to fly or shoot lasers from your eyes, but you'll have a heart as strong as The Hulk and the immune system of someone who's never heard of the common cold.

The Social Butterfly Effect

Being happy makes you more likable (or possibly hated by consistently unhappy people). It's like having a magnetic personality that attracts people to you. Suddenly, you're the life of the party, the go-to person for advice, and everyone wants to sit next to you at lunch. Picture yourself as a social butterfly, flitting from one flower of friendship to another, sipping the nectar of human connection. And yes, I did compare social interaction to flower nectar. Go with it.

Enhanced Problem-Solving Skills (Or How to Become a Puzzle Master)

When you're happy, your brain works better. It's like your mind goes from being an outdated computer running Windows 95 to the latest, super-fast, ultra-efficient model. You can solve problems faster, think more clearly, and develop innovative solutions that would make Einstein nod in approval. So, next time you're stuck in a tricky situation, try watching a funny cat video or telling a joke. You'll be amazed at how quickly your brain shifts into high gear.

The Ripple Effect of Happiness

Your happiness doesn't just impact you; it ripples out to everyone around you. It's like tossing a pebble into a pond and watching the waves spread out. When you're happy, you make your family happier, your friends more cheerful, and even your pets perkier. Yes, even your dog notices when you're happy, making them wag their tail even harder. Happiness is a gift that keeps on giving, spreading joy far and wide.

Essential Strategies for Enhancing Individual Happiness

In the pursuit of happiness, individuals often find themselves entangled in a myriad of self-help books, therapies, and philosophical doctrines. Yet, the simplicity of happiness usually eludes us, caught up in complex life dynamics. Enhancing individual happiness is a multifaceted endeavor that involves various aspects of life. This chapter outlines practical, research-backed strategies designed to improve individual happiness. The approaches here are structured around cultivating a balanced life that values mindfulness, meaningful relationships, personal goals, and emotional resilience.

1. Cultivate Mindfulness and Presence

Mindfulness—the art of being fully present in the moment—has been shown to boost happiness levels significantly. It encourages an appreciation of the present, reducing worries about the past and anxieties about the future.

Strategy:

- **Daily Meditation:** Start with as little as five minutes a day. Use guided meditations if beginning or maintaining focus is challenging.
- **Mindful Walking:** Turn routine walks into mindfulness exercises by focusing on the sensation of movement and the environment around you.

2. Foster Meaningful Relationships

Humans are inherently social creatures, and strong, healthy relationships are foundational to our well-being. Research suggests that the quality of our relationships is more predictive of happiness than the quantity.

Strategy:

- **Regular Check-ins:** Make it a habit to regularly reach out to friends and family, whether through messaging, calls, or in-person meetings.

- **Community Engagement:** Join clubs, groups, or online forums that align with your interests to build connections and foster a sense of belonging.

3. Pursue Achievable Goals

Goal setting is not just about achieving career milestones or personal records; it's also about growth and fulfillment. Setting and achieving realistic goals can lead to significant satisfaction and happiness.

Strategy:

- **SMART Goals:** Set Specific, Measurable, Achievable, Relevant, and Time-bound goals that motivate you without causing undue stress.
- **Celebrate Small Wins:** Recognize and celebrate the small achievements along the way. This builds momentum and positivity.

4. Develop Emotional Resilience

The ability to bounce back from setbacks is crucial for sustained happiness. Emotional resilience does not mean avoiding sadness or disappointment but instead developing the ability to cope effectively.

Strategy:

- **Reflective Journaling:** Regularly write down your thoughts and feelings, especially during difficult times, to process emotions constructively.

- **Seek Feedback:** Embrace constructive criticism and use it to grow. Surround yourself with people who can provide honest, compassionate feedback.

5. Practice Gratitude

Gratitude is powerfully associated with greater happiness. Acknowledging the good in your life—even during times of hardship—can foster resilience, improve relationships, and reduce stress.

Strategy:

- **Gratitude Journal:** Keep a daily log of things you are grateful for, no matter how small. This can shift your focus from what's missing to what's abundant.
- **Gratitude Letters:** Occasionally write letters to people who have positively impacted your life, expressing your appreciation.

6. Prioritize Physical Health

Physical well-being is inextricably linked to mental health. Regular exercise, adequate sleep, and a nutritious diet can elevate mood and energy levels, thereby enhancing overall happiness.

Strategy:

- **Incorporate Activity:** Find a form of exercise you enjoy and can consistently engage in, whether it's yoga, dancing, or simple daily walks.
- **Sleep Hygiene:** Establish a calming bedtime routine and aim for 7-9 hours of sleep per night to improve mood and cognitive function.

7. Develop Relationships

Foster strong connections with family, friends, and community members. Meaningful relationships contribute significantly to overall happiness and well-being.

Strategy:

- **Educate yourself** on different cultures, customs, and courtesies.
- **Find some commonalities** you have with colleagues
- **Diversify** your hobbies.

8. Engage in Acts of Kindness:

Helping others can boost your mood and provide a sense of purpose. Volunteer work or simple acts of kindness in your daily life can make a difference.

Strategy:

- **Pay It Forward:** This could be as simple as paying for the person's coffee in line behind you at a café. Such a surprise can brighten someone's day and inspire them to continue the chain of kindness.
- **Compliment Someone:** Offering a genuine compliment can significantly lift someone's spirits. Whether it's praising a colleague's work or a stranger's outfit, it can make a big difference in their day.
- **Leave a Generous Tip:** This is especially important when you notice the server or service provider has had a tough day or did an exceptional job.
- **Send Unexpected Notes:** Write a note of appreciation or encouragement and leave it for someone to find, or mail it to an old friend.

- **Help Someone in Need:** If you see someone struggling with groceries or needing help crossing the street, offering your assistance is a simple yet powerful gesture.
- **Volunteer Regularly:** Find a local charity or community organization that resonates with your values and commit to volunteering. Regular service is deeply fulfilling, whether helping at a food bank, tutoring children, or working with senior citizens.

9. Engage in Activities You Enjoy

Make time for hobbies and activities that bring you joy and fulfillment. Whether painting, playing music, hiking, or gardening, doing what you love is essential for happiness.

Strategy:

- **Integrate Interests into Your Daily Schedule:** Making time for activities you love can be challenging, especially with a busy schedule.
- **Try New Things:** Periodically choose new activities to try. This could be something you've always wanted to do, like a cooking class, learning a new language, or trying out a sport. New activities can be exciting and enriching.
- **Join Clubs or Groups:** Look for clubs or groups that align with your interests. Whether it's a book club, hiking group, or photography guild, being part of a community with similar interests can enhance your engagement and provide social support.
- **Set Challenges or Goals:** Give yourself small challenges or set goals related to your hobbies. For example, if you enjoy cycling, set a goal to complete a certain distance each month. If you're into photography, challenge yourself to capture photos from

different genres each month. This keeps your engagement active and provides a sense of achievement.
- **Share Your Hobby:** Sharing your interest with others can also enhance your enjoyment. Teach a skill you've mastered, share your craft on social media, or present your work in community exhibitions. Sharing can provide feedback and new perspectives that reinvigorate your passion.

10. Seek Professional Help if Needed

If you're struggling with persistent feelings of unhappiness or mental health issues, don't hesitate to seek support from a therapist or counselor.

Seeking professional help for mental health, personal development, or life challenges is a vital step toward enhancing well-being. Here are two strategies to effectively find and utilize professional assistance:

Strategy:

- **Finding the Right Professional:** The effectiveness of professional help often depends on how well the professional's expertise aligns with your needs and how comfortable you feel with them. Here's how you can find the right professional for your needs:
    - **Research Options:** Start by understanding the type of professional who might best address your needs. This might be a psychologist, psychiatrist, or licensed mental health counselor. For career guidance, a career coach or mentor might be ideal. Use trusted resources to find qualified professionals, such as referrals from your doctor, recommendations from trusted friends, or reputable websites.

- **Check Credentials and Reviews:** Ensure the professionals you consider are appropriately credentialed and licensed. Look for reviews or testimonials from previous clients to gauge their effectiveness and approach.
- **Schedule a Consultation:** Many professionals offer a preliminary consultation, sometimes at no cost. Use this as an opportunity to ask about their experience with issues similar to yours, their approach, and what you can expect from the sessions. This meeting can help you determine if you feel comfortable with their style and demeanor.
- **Consider Logistics:** Think about factors such as location, availability, and cost. Some professionals offer virtual sessions, which can be convenient if time or distance is a concern. Also, check if your health insurance covers their services or if they offer a sliding scale for payment based on income.

- **Maximizing the Benefits of Professional Help:** Once you find the right professional, it's essential to actively engage in the process to get the most out of it:
  - **Set Clear Goals:** Before beginning your sessions, consider what you hope to achieve. Discuss these goals with your professional to ensure they understand your expectations and can tailor their approach accordingly.
  - **Be Open and Honest:** The more open you can be about your feelings and experiences, the more your therapist or coach can help you. It might be uncomfortable to share personal details, but transparency is crucial for practical help.
  - **Do the Work Outside Sessions:** Often, professionals will suggest exercises or practices to do between sessions.

Commit to these activities, designed to help you progress toward your goals.

- **Evaluate Progress:** Periodically assess whether you're making progress with the help of your professional. Discuss this with them if you feel you're not getting the desired results. It may be necessary to adjust your goals or their methods, or in some cases, consider a different professional.
- **Consider Long-term Engagement:** Sometimes, especially for complex issues, long-term engagement might be necessary. Be prepared that some types of growth and healing can take time, and realistic expectations are crucial.

Conclusion

Happiness is not a static state but a dynamic process of engaging positively with life. Individuals can significantly enhance their personal happiness by cultivating mindfulness, fostering meaningful relationships, pursuing achievable goals, developing emotional resilience, practicing gratitude, and prioritizing physical health. Remember, the path to happiness is as personal as your fingerprints. Explore these strategies, adapt them to your needs, and watch your life transform, one joyful step at a time.

Individual happiness is like the secret sauce that makes life delicious. It boosts productivity, improves health, enhances social interactions, and turns you into a problem-solving machine. Plus, it's just plain fun to be happy. So, embrace your inner joy, laugh often, and spread happiness wherever you go. Because in the grand circus of life, being happy makes you the star performer everyone loves to watch. And who doesn't want to be the star of their own show?

Reflection Questions

What activities, people, or environments consistently bring you the most joy and fulfillment, and how can you incorporate more of these into your daily life?

What are your life's primary sources of stress or dissatisfaction, and what steps can you take to address or mitigate these challenges?

How do your personal goals and values align with your daily activities and choices, and what changes can you make to ensure a better alignment?

How do your relationships with family, friends, and colleagues impact your overall happiness, and what actions can you take to strengthen these connections and foster a supportive community?

CHAPTER 7

OVERCOMING CHALLENGES OF AN UNHAPPY WORKPLACE: A FUN GUIDE TO BOOSTING PRODUCTIVITY

Welcome to the Unhappy Workplace, where tears are part of the dress code and stress-induced hair loss is considered a badge of honor. If you've ever thought about running away to join the circus because it seems more stable than your 9-to-5, you're not alone. But fear not, weary worker! We're here to explore the absurdity of our office woes and find laughable yet effective ways to transform that dismal desk job into a place of productivity and maybe even joy.

The Daily Grind: Navigating the Office Jungle

The Monday Blues

Every week starts with Monday, a day as universally loved as soggy whole wheat cereal. The first step in tackling workplace unhappiness is accepting that Monday will always be there, like an unpaid intern who won't leave. So why not make it fun? Treat Monday like a bizarre holiday. Wear something ridiculous to work, like mismatched socks that no one can see, a Hawaiian shirt, or a tiara. Even better, declare it "Cake Day." Nothing beats workplace misery like a sugar rush at 9 AM.

The Soul-Sucking Staff Meeting

Meetings are the office equivalent of purgatory. You're not quite dead, but you're not really living either. The next time you're stuck in a two-hour debate about which office is not meeting their suspense or a task that no one wants to do, but we all agree upon when the boss asks, bring a bingo card. Populate it with classic phrases like "circle back," "touch base," "late," "mission," and "low-hanging fruit." Not only will it keep you entertained, but it might just inject a bit of competitive spirit into the room. The winner gets to pick the meeting snacks next time—hello, Cake Day!

The Passive-Aggressive Post-It Notes

Ah, the Post-It note: the weapon of choice for the passive-aggressive office warrior. Instead of getting bogged down by these paper provocations, turn them into a game. Create a "Post-It Note Wall of Fame" where you display the most creatively passive-aggressive notes for all to see. Give out monthly awards. The winner gets a golden pen and a book on conflict resolution—because we all know they need it.

Coping with Coworkers: Love 'Em or Leave 'Em (Just Not in a Creepy Way)

Morning Maniac
There's one in every office: the person who arrives at work as if they've just downed a triple espresso and seen a unicorn on the way in. Their relentless cheeriness is a direct assault on your pre-caffeine state. Counteract their enthusiasm with absurd levels of sarcasm. When they greet you with "Good morning!" respond with, "Oh, is it? I hadn't noticed." It won't make them any less cheery, but it will at least make you feel better.

The Lunch Looter
Nothing says "I respect you," like stealing your coworker's lunch. If you're dealing with a serial food thief, it's time to get creative. Label your lunch with increasingly bizarre warnings: "Caution: I lick my bread" or "Delicious Diuretic Delight." Alternatively, pack decoy lunches with questionable ingredients—who wouldn't want a mayonnaise and jelly sandwich or a sardine oil smoothie? You'll be the lunchroom legend by the time they figure out the ruse.

Personal Space Cadet
Some people love being in your personal space or just too touchy-feely. If you're not into unsolicited hugs from Henry in HR or Margaret in Marketing, develop a reputation for awkwardness. When Anna from Accounting comes in for a hug, do something unexpected: pat her on the head, shake her hand vigorously, or pretend you didn't notice and walk away. Anna will soon realize you're a high-risk hug and move on to more receptive targets.

Tackling the Terrible Boss: Surviving the Tyranny

The Micromanager

The micromanager is convinced you're incapable of doing anything without their input. Beat them at their own game by providing overly detailed updates. "Just sent an email. I followed up with a phone call, but there was no answer. Now awaiting a response. Deciding between a red or blue pen for my notes. Leaning towards red. Might do blue after all." Eventually, they'll realize they don't need to know about your every move and back off—or they'll go insane. Either way, mission accomplished.

The Phantom Boss

Contrary to the micromanager, the phantom boss is never around when you need them. Turn their absence into a game of hide-and-seek. Leave cryptic messages on their desks, like "We've all gone to a remote island for an impromptu team-building exercise. Hope you can join us!" or "We had steak and lobster catered for lunch again." This will either prompt them to be more present or lead to a delightful mystery-solving adventure when they return.

The Overgrown Toddler

Some bosses throw tantrums when things don't go their way. Keep a pack of juice boxes and some cookies handy. When the boss starts to lose it, offer them a snack. "Looks like someone's having a rough day. How about a juice?" The sheer absurdity of the gesture will either calm them down or leave them speechless—both are wins.

Creating a Happier Environment: Guerrilla Tactics for Office Joy

The Office Prankster
Sometimes, the best way to cope with a dreary workplace is to embrace your inner prankster. Replace the boss's stapler with a toy one that squeaks. Cover a coworker's desk in sticky notes. Fill the break room with balloons. Pranks should be safe, harmless, and funny, not mean-spirited. The key is to keep everyone laughing, even when it's at their own expense.

The Secret Complimenter
In a world where criticism flows freely, be the secret complimenter. Leave anonymous notes of appreciation for your coworkers. "You rocked that presentation today!" or "Your laugh brightens this office." The mystery and positivity will lift spirits and create a more supportive atmosphere.

The Makeover
Transform your workspace into a personal oasis. Decorate with photos, quirky knick-knacks, or even a tiny Zen garden. A little slice of personal heaven can make the daily grind more bearable. Plus, it's a great conversation starter—nothing says "I'm interesting" like a desk goldfish named Bulldog.

The Bigger Picture: Finding Purpose in the Madness

Monotony Makeover

Sometimes, the most unbearable tasks can be seen in a new light. Instead of thinking of that data entry as soul-crushing, imagine you're a secret agent inputting top-secret information. Those endless emails? They're your way of communicating with distant allies in the fight against boredom. By reframing the mundane, you can find a bit of joy in the ridiculous.

Celebrate the Small Wins

Did you finally get the printer to work? Celebrate! Did you find the last working stapler? You didn't lose a pen this week! Throw a mini-party! By acknowledging and celebrating small victories, you create a culture of positivity. Plus, it's a great excuse to have more cake, and who doesn't love cake?

Have an Out

Have something to look forward to outside of work. Plan a weekend getaway, a fun evening with friends, or a hobby you love. Have a countdown calendar. Knowing there's something enjoyable waiting for you can make the workday feel less like a life sentence.

The Final Frontier: Embracing the Absurd

Office Olympics
Channel your inner athlete with the Office Olympics. Events can include the Chair Race, the Paper Airplane Throw, and the Rubber Band Archery. Not only does it break up the monotony, but it fosters teamwork and camaraderie. Just don't get too competitive—nobody needs an injury report from the Rubber Band Archery finals.

Themed Workdays
Spice up the workweek with themed days. Crazy Hat Day, Pajama Day, or Dress Like Your Boss Day (this one's especially fun if your boss has a distinct style). Themes give everyone something to laugh about and look forward to, making the office feel less like a grind and more like a bizarre sitcom.

Create a "Wall of Shame
Embrace the mistakes and mishaps with a "Wall of Shame." Encourage coworkers to post their funniest work fails (anonymously if they prefer). Whether it's a typo in an extensive report or a hilarious email mishap, celebrating these moments can help everyone feel more human and less stressed about perfection.

Conclusion: The Power of Humor in the Workplace

Ultimately, the power of humor is the key to overcoming the challenges of an unhappy workplace. By finding ways to laugh at the absurdity of office life, you can transform a place of dread into a playground of productivity. It's about making the most of the situation, finding joy in the little things, and not taking everything so seriously.

Remember, the workplace is just a stage; we're all actors in a never-ending office sitcom. So embrace the quirks, laugh at the nonsense, and turn those workplace woes into opportunities for fun. After all, if you can't laugh at the chaos, you might end up crying into your keyboard—and nobody wants that.

So, next time you feel the weight of the office bearing down on you, take a deep breath, put on your imaginary clown shoes, and turn that frown upside down. Welcome to the happier, more productive workplace. It's not just a job—it's a comedy show. Enjoy the performance!

Reflection Questions

What factors or situations in your workplace contribute most significantly to your unhappiness? How can you address these issues directly or adapt your perspective to mitigate their impact?

How effective is your communication with colleagues and supervisors? What steps can you take to improve your interpersonal relationships and foster a more positive and supportive work environment?

What personal strategies and coping mechanisms can you implement to manage stress and maintain your well-being in the face of workplace challenges? How can you create a balance between work demands and your personal needs?

CHAPTER 8

SUCCESSFUL COMPANIES EMBRACING HAPPINESS

Ensuring happiness in the workplace is increasingly becoming a strategic priority for companies around the globe. Recognizing that a happy workforce is a more productive, creative, and loyal one, businesses are investing heavily in initiatives designed to enhance employee well-being. Here are several ways companies are planning to ensure happiness in the workplace in the future:

1. Flexible Work Arrangements

Flexible work arrangements are at the forefront of workplace happiness strategies. The COVID-19 pandemic has accelerated the adoption of remote work, and companies are expected to continue offering flexible work options, including remote work, hybrid models, and flexible hours. These arrangements allow employees to balance their personal and professional lives better, reducing stress and increasing job satisfaction.

Case Study: Google and Microsoft

Companies like Google and Microsoft have introduced hybrid work models where employees can work from home or come to the office. This flexibility helps employees manage their work-life balance effectively. Here's how each company has approached this transition:

Google

Flexible Work Schedule:

- **Remote Work Options**: Google offers employees the flexibility to work remotely for a significant portion of the week. Employees can work from home two or three days a week.
- **Work-from-Anywhere Weeks:** Google allows employees to work from any location for up to four weeks a year, allowing for greater personal flexibility.

Office Redesigns:

- **Collaboration Spaces:** Google's offices are being redesigned to support hybrid work, with more spaces for collaboration and fewer individual desks.

- **Hot Desking:** Implementation of shared workstations that employees can reserve as needed, supporting a more fluid use of office space.

Technology and Tools:

- **Google Workspace Enhancements:** Improvements to Google Workspace (formerly G Suite) to better support remote collaboration, including enhancements to Google Meet, Docs, and other productivity tools.

Health and Safety Measures:

- **Enhanced Sanitation and Safety Protocols:** Offices have been upgraded with new safety measures to protect employees who choose to work on-site, such as increased cleaning protocols and social distancing guidelines.

Microsoft

Flexible Work Policy:

- **Hybrid Work Guidelines:** Microsoft has implemented guidelines that allow employees to work from home up to 50% of the time. Managers have the discretion to approve additional remote workdays.
- **Remote Work by Default:** For specific roles and positions, remote work can be the default setup, providing maximum flexibility for employees.

Workplace Modernization:

- **Dynamic Office Spaces:** Microsoft is redesigning offices to support hybrid work, emphasizing spaces for team collaboration and meetings over traditional desk setups.
- **Worksite Reservations:** Implementing systems that allow employees to book office space when they plan to come in, ensuring efficient use of the office environment.

Technological Support:

- **Microsoft Teams:** Microsoft Teams has been continuously enhanced, integrating new features to support virtual meetings, collaboration, and productivity.
- **Cloud Services:** Emphasis on cloud solutions like Azure to ensure seamless access to work resources from anywhere.

Employee Well-being:

- **Focus on Mental Health:** Initiatives to support employee well-being, including mental health days, counseling services, and resources to manage work-life balance.
- **Physical Health and Safety:** Implementing health checks, contact tracing, and other measures to ensure a safe work environment for those returning to the office.

Common Initiatives

- **Hybrid Meeting Solutions:** Both companies are investing in technologies that enhance the hybrid meeting experience, ensuring remote participants have an equal presence in meetings through advanced video conferencing tools and meeting room setups.

- **Learning and Development:** Offering extensive training programs to help employees and managers adapt to hybrid work, including best practices for remote work, collaboration tools training, and leadership development for managing distributed teams.
- **Feedback Mechanisms:** Regularly soliciting employee feedback to refine and improve hybrid work policies, ensuring that they meet the evolving needs of their workforce.

By implementing these strategies, Google and Microsoft aim to create a flexible and efficient work environment that supports productivity, collaboration, and employee well-being in the hybrid era.

2. Mental Health and Wellness Programs

Mental health is becoming a critical focus for ensuring workplace happiness. Companies are increasingly recognizing the importance of mental well-being and are implementing comprehensive wellness programs that include mental health support. This may involve providing access to therapy, mental health days, stress management workshops, and creating an open culture around mental health discussions.

Case Study: Salesforce

Salesforce has recognized the importance of mental health and counseling for its employees and has implemented several initiatives and programs to support their well-being. Here are some ways Salesforce has incorporated mental health and counseling:

- **Employee Assistance Programs (EAPs):** Salesforce offers EAPs that provide confidential counseling and mental health support to employees and their families. These programs typically include access to licensed professionals for personal or work-related issues.
- **Wellness Reimbursement Program**: Salesforce provides a wellness reimbursement program through which employees can be reimbursed for expenses related to mental health and well-being activities. These can include therapy sessions, mental health apps, and other related services.
- **Mindfulness and Meditation Programs**: Salesforce has implemented mindfulness and meditation programs to help employees manage stress and improve their mental well-being. These programs often include guided sessions, workshops, and access to meditation apps.
- **Mental Health Days:** Understanding the need for time off to focus on mental health, Salesforce encourages employees

to take mental health days when needed. This helps reduce burnout and supports overall mental wellness.
- **Training for Managers:** Salesforce provides managers with training to recognize signs of mental health issues among their team members and approach these situations with empathy and support. This training helps create a supportive work environment.
- **Mental Health Awareness Campaigns:** Salesforce runs internal campaigns to raise awareness about mental health issues and reduce stigma. These campaigns often include sharing resources and personal stories and promoting open conversations about mental health.
- **Partnerships with Mental Health Organizations**: Salesforce collaborates with mental health organizations to provide employees with resources and support. These partnerships can include access to mental health platforms, expert talks, and workshops.
- **Flexible Work Arrangements:** By offering flexible work arrangements, including remote work options, Salesforce helps employees balance their work and personal lives, which can positively impact mental health.
- **Health and Wellness Hubs:** Salesforce has established health and wellness hubs in some of its offices, providing a dedicated space for employees to access wellness resources, counseling services, and relaxation areas.
- **Regular Employee Surveys and Feedback:** To continuously improve their mental health initiatives, Salesforce conducts regular surveys and collects employee feedback on their mental health needs and the effectiveness of current programs.

These initiatives demonstrate Salesforce's commitment to fostering a supportive work environment that prioritizes its employees' mental health and well-being.

3. Employee Engagement and Recognition

Engagement and recognition are vital components of a happy workplace. Companies are investing in platforms and programs that recognize and reward employee achievements, both big and small. Regular feedback, employee appreciation days, and peer recognition programs help create a culture where employees feel valued and motivated.

Case Study: Adobe's "Check-In" System

Adobe's "Check-In" system replaces annual performance reviews with ongoing feedback and recognition, fostering a more engaged and satisfied workforce. This system has fostered a more involved workforce through several key elements:

Continuous Feedback

- **Regular Conversations:** Adobe's "Check In" encourages regular, informal conversations between employees and managers rather than once-a-year reviews. This helps employees receive timely feedback and guidance.
- **Real-Time Adjustments:** Continuous feedback allows employees to make real-time adjustments to their performance, aligning more closely with organizational goals and expectations.

Employee Development

- **Personal Growth Focus:** The system emphasizes personal and professional growth over merely evaluating past performance. Managers are encouraged to discuss career aspirations, skill development, and future opportunities with employees.
- **Customized Goals:** Employees can set and adjust goals more frequently, ensuring they remain relevant and aligned with personal development and organizational needs.

Empowerment and Ownership

- **Employee Involvement**: Employees are more involved in the process, with opportunities to initiate check-ins and provide input on their performance and development needs.
- **Self-Assessment**: The system often includes a self-assessment component, promoting self-reflection and a sense of ownership over one's career trajectory.

Reduction of Anxiety and Stress

- **Elimination of Ratings**: By eliminating traditional performance ratings, Adobe reduced the anxiety and stress associated with annual reviews. This helps create a more positive and supportive work environment.
- **Constructive Conversations**: The focus on regular, constructive conversations helps build stronger relationships between employees and managers, fostering trust and open communication.

Flexibility and Adaptability

- **Agile Goal Setting**: Employees can set short-term goals and adapt them as priorities change, making the system more agile and responsive to the dynamic nature of work.
- **Tailored Feedback**: Feedback is more tailored and specific to recent work, making it more relevant and actionable.

Increased Engagement and Motivation

- **Recognition of Achievements**: Regular check-ins allow for more frequent recognition of achievements and contributions, boosting morale and motivation.

- **Clear Expectations**: Ongoing dialogue ensures that employees understand expectations and how their work contributes to the organization's success.

Enhanced Collaboration

- **Team Alignment**: Continuous check-ins help ensure team members are aligned with each other and broader organizational goals, enhancing collaboration and teamwork.
- **Open Communication Culture**: The system fosters a culture of open communication, where feedback is a two-way street, and employees feel heard and valued.

Adobe's "Check In" system promotes a more engaged workforce by making performance management a continuous, collaborative, and supportive process that focuses on growth, development, and real-time feedback.

4. Career Development Opportunities

Providing opportunities for growth and development is crucial for employee happiness. Companies are focusing on creating clear career paths, offering professional development programs, and supporting continuous learning. This not only helps employees advance their careers but also keeps them engaged and motivated.

Case Study: LinkedIn

LinkedIn offers its employees access to LinkedIn Learning, an online platform with thousands of courses on various topics, ensuring continuous professional development and career growth.

5. Inclusive and Diverse Work Environments

Diversity and inclusion are key drivers of workplace happiness. Companies are striving to create inclusive cultures where all employees feel respected and valued regardless of their background. This involves implementing diversity training, establishing employee resource groups (ERGs), and promoting policies that support diversity and inclusion.

Case Study: IBM

IBM has long been a leader in diversity and inclusion, offering various ERGs, mentoring programs, and diversity training to ensure an inclusive workplace environment. Their goal is to ensure that IBM leverages the full potential of its workforce, fostering innovation and driving business success by valuing diverse perspectives and creating an environment where everyone can thrive. Here are some key elements of IBM's D&I program:

- **Leadership Commitment**: IBM's leadership is deeply committed to diversity and inclusion, with senior executives playing a critical role in driving the agenda. The company's CEO and senior leaders frequently communicate the importance of D&I and are actively involved in initiatives to promote an inclusive culture.
- **Employee Resource Groups (ERGs)**: IBM supports various ERGs, which are voluntary, employee-led groups that foster a diverse and inclusive workplace aligned with the organization's mission, values, goals, and business practices. ERGs provide a platform for employees to connect, share experiences, and advocate for initiatives that support their communities.
- **Inclusive Hiring Practices**: IBM has established inclusive hiring practices to attract diverse talent. This includes partnerships with organizations focusing on underrepresented groups, im-

plementing bias-free recruitment processes, and ensuring diverse interview panels.

- **Training and Education:** IBM offers extensive training and education programs to raise awareness and build skills related to diversity and inclusion. This includes unconscious bias training, inclusive leadership training, and cultural competency workshops.
- **Flexible Work Policies:** To support a diverse workforce, IBM provides flexible work policies that accommodate different needs and lifestyles. This includes remote work options, flexible hours, and comprehensive benefits that support work-life balance.
- **Equal Pay and Advancement Opportunities:** IBM is committed to ensuring equal pay for equal work and providing equal opportunities for advancement. The company regularly reviews compensation practices and career development programs to eliminate disparities and promote fairness.
- **Supplier Diversity:** IBM's supplier diversity program seeks to promote the inclusion of diverse suppliers in its procurement processes. The company works with businesses owned by minorities, women, veterans, LGBTQ+ individuals, and people with disabilities to ensure they have opportunities to compete for contracts.
- **Data-Driven Approach:** IBM uses data and analytics to measure the effectiveness of its D&I initiatives. This includes tracking representation metrics, conducting employee surveys, and analyzing the impact of D&I programs on business outcomes.
- **Global Perspective:** IBM's D&I program has a global reach, addressing diversity and inclusion issues in different regions and cultures. The company tailors its initiatives to meet the unique needs of its global workforce, ensuring relevance and effectiveness across different markets.

- **Community Engagement:** IBM engages with the broader community through partnerships, sponsorships, and volunteer initiatives that promote diversity and inclusion. This includes supporting educational programs, advocacy groups, and other organizations working towards social equity.

Overall, IBM's Diversity and Inclusion program is a multifaceted approach aimed at creating a workplace where everyone feels valued and empowered to contribute to their fullest potential. This commitment not only enhances the employee experience but also drives innovation and business success.

6. Work-Life Balance Initiatives

Work-life balance is a significant factor in employee happiness. Companies are introducing initiatives such as flexible work hours, unlimited paid time off (PTO), parental leave, and on-site childcare to help employees balance their personal and professional lives.

Case Study: Netflix

Netflix is known for its unique corporate culture, which emphasizes freedom and responsibility. Netflix offers unlimited PTO, allowing employees to take as much time off as they need, trusting them to manage their time effectively, and ensuring they have the flexibility to balance work and personal life. Their approach to work-life balance is unconventional and revolves around several fundamental principles:

- **No Set Vacation Policy:** Netflix offers an unlimited vacation policy, where employees can take as much time off as they feel necessary. The company trusts employees to manage their own time and performance and to take time off when they need it without seeking approval from managers.

- **Flexible Work Hours:** Netflix does not have strict work hours, allowing employees to choose their schedules. This flexibility helps employees more effectively balance their work and personal lives.
- **Focus on Results:** The company focuses on results rather than the number of hours worked. Employees are evaluated based on their contributions and achievements rather than their presence in the office or adherence to a set schedule.
- **Empowerment and Responsibility:** Netflix empowers employees by giving them significant responsibility and expecting them to make decisions in the company's best interest. This trust-based approach encourages a sense of ownership and accountability, which can positively impact work-life balance.
- **Supportive Work Environment:** Netflix strives to create a supportive work environment that promotes mental and physical well-being. This includes offering resources for stress management, encouraging regular breaks, and fostering a culture of open communication.
- **Parental Leave:** Netflix provides generous parental leave policies, allowing new parents to take ample time off to care for their newborns. This policy is part of their broader commitment to supporting employees' family lives.
- **Health and Wellness Programs:** The company offers various health and wellness programs to support employees' physical and mental health. These programs include access to fitness facilities, wellness workshops, and mental health resources.

While Netflix's work-life balance initiatives may not be conventional, they align with the company's overall culture of freedom, responsibility, and high performance. By giving employees control over their time and focusing on results, Netflix aims to create a work environment where individuals can professionally and personally thrive.

7. Health and Fitness Programs

Physical health is closely linked to mental well-being and overall happiness. Companies are implementing health and fitness programs, including on-site gyms, fitness classes, health screenings, and wellness challenges, to encourage a healthy lifestyle among employees.

Case Study: Google

Google provides employees access to on-site fitness centers, healthy meals, and wellness programs to promote a healthy lifestyle and well-being. Google's on-site fitness centers are part of the company's effort to encourage employee wellness and work-life balance. These fitness centers are state-of-the-art facilities designed to help employees maintain their physical health and well-being. Here are some key features and benefits of Google's on-site fitness centers:

Comprehensive Facilities

- **Gym Equipment:** They are equipped with a wide range of gym equipment, including cardio machines (treadmills, ellipticals, bikes), strength training equipment (free weights, weight machines), and functional fitness tools.
- **Sports Facilities:** Some centers include courts for basketball, volleyball, and tennis, swimming pools, and climbing walls.

Group Classes

- Google offers a variety of group fitness classes such as yoga, Pilates, spinning, Zumba, and high-intensity interval training (HIIT).
- Classes are led by professional instructors designed to accommodate different fitness levels.

Personal Training

- Employees can access personal training services for individualized fitness plans and guidance.
- Trainers help set fitness goals, create personalized workouts, and provide motivation and support.

Wellness Programs

- The fitness centers often host wellness programs that include activities like meditation, mindfulness training, and stress management workshops.
- These programs are designed to support overall mental and emotional well-being.

Convenience

- The on-site fitness centers provide a convenient way for employees to integrate exercise into their daily routines without leaving the workplace.
- Many centers are open for extended hours, making it easier for employees to work out before, after, or during breaks.

Community and Social Engagement

- The fitness centers serve as a social hub where employees can meet and interact with colleagues from different departments.
- This helps build a sense of community and enhances team bonding.

Health Incentives

Google often encourages participation in fitness activities by offering health incentives, such as fitness challenges and rewards for meeting certain activity milestones.

Overall, Google's on-site fitness centers are a vital component of their employee benefits package, contributing to a healthier, happier, and more productive workforce.

8. Employee Autonomy and Empowerment

Giving employees autonomy and empowering them to make decisions can significantly enhance their happiness at work. Companies are fostering environments where employees have the freedom to innovate, make decisions, and take ownership of their work.

Case Study: Spotify

Spotify's "Agile" working model, often referred to as the "Spotify Model," allows employees to self-organize into teams, giving them the autonomy to decide how they work best and fostering a sense of ownership and empowerment. It emphasizes autonomy, collaboration, and alignment within a flexible and dynamic framework. Here are the key elements and principles of the Spotify Model:

Squads

- **Definition:** Squads are small, cross-functional teams, similar to Scrum teams.
- **Structure:** Each squad is responsible for a specific aspect of the product and operates autonomously, with the freedom to choose their own way of working.

- **Roles:** Squads typically include all the necessary roles, such as developers, designers, and product owners, to deliver their pieces of the product.

Tribes

- **Definition:** Tribes are collections of squads that work in related areas.
- **Purpose:** They help manage dependencies and facilitate communication and collaboration between squads.
- **Size:** A tribe usually consists of up to 100 people to maintain a community feeling.

Chapters

- **Definition:** Chapters are groups of individuals from different squads within the same tribe who have similar skills or roles.
- **Purpose:** Chapters ensure that practices and standards are consistent across squads. They provide a forum for knowledge sharing and professional development.

Guilds

- **Definition:** Guilds are voluntary, cross-tribe communities of interest.
- **Purpose:** They allow people with a shared interest in a particular area (e.g., web development, testing) to share knowledge, practices, and tools across the organization.

Roles within the Model

- **Product Owner:** Focuses on maximizing product value and managing the backlog for the squad.

- **Agile Coach:** Supports squads in adopting and improving agile practices and facilitating continuous improvement.

Culture and Mindset

- **Autonomy:** Squads can decide how they work to achieve their goals.
- **Alignment:** Despite the autonomy, there's a strong focus on ensuring all teams are aligned with the overall company vision and objectives.
- **Servant Leadership:** Leaders serve their teams by removing obstacles and supporting their needs rather than directing their work.

Processes and Practices

- **Lean Principles:** Emphasis on eliminating waste, optimizing processes, and continuous improvement.
- **Iterative Development:** Work is broken down into small, manageable pieces, allowing for regular feedback and adjustments.
- **Continuous Delivery:** Frequent, reliable releases through automated testing and deployment.

Tools and Techniques

- **Data-Driven Decision Making:** Extensive use of data and metrics to guide decisions and measure progress.
- **Retrospectives and Feedback Loops:** Regular sessions to reflect on processes and outcomes, fostering a culture of continuous improvement.

Benefits of the Spotify Model

- **Innovation and Speed:** Increased autonomy and reduced dependencies allow for faster innovation and delivery.
- **Employee Satisfaction:** Empowering teams and fostering a culture of trust and responsibility leads to higher job satisfaction.
- **Scalability:** The model is designed to scale effectively with the organization's growth while maintaining agility.

Challenges

- **Coordination and Alignment:** Ensuring alignment across autonomous teams can be challenging.
- **Consistency:** Maintaining consistent standards and practices across different squads and tribes requires ongoing effort.

The Spotify Model has inspired many organizations to adapt their Agile practices to better fit their unique contexts.

9. Positive Work Culture

A positive work culture is essential for employee happiness. Companies are focusing on building cultures based on trust, respect, collaboration, and open communication. This involves fostering a supportive environment where employees feel comfortable expressing themselves and collaborating with others.

Case Study: Zappos

Zappos is known for its unique and positive company culture, emphasizing core values such as delivering happiness, embracing change, and creating fun and a little weirdness in the workplace. Here are some of the fun and weird things they do in the workplace to keep the environment lively and engaging:

Parades and Costume Contests

- **Random Parades:** Employees might spontaneously hold parades in the office, complete with music and costumes.
- **Costume Contests:** Zappos frequently holds costume contests where employees dress up according to themes, often coinciding with holidays or special events.

Office Decorations

- **Themed Workspaces:** Departments often have themed decorations, from pirate ships to jungle setups, making each area unique and fun.
- **Personalized Cubicles:** Employees are encouraged to decorate their workspaces in any way they like, reflecting their personalities and interests.

Fun Committees and Clubs

- **Culture Club:** This employee-led group organizes events, celebrations, and activities to promote a fun work environment.
- **Fun Committees:** Various committees are responsible for planning and executing fun events, from game nights to talent shows.

Spontaneous Celebrations

- **Bell Ringing:** When a significant milestone is reached, such as a big sale or project completion, a bell is rung, and everyone celebrates.
- **Surprise Parties:** Random surprise parties are held to celebrate achievements, birthdays, or just because.

Employee Engagement Activities

- **Games and Competitions:** Regular games and competitions are held, including trivia, scavenger hunts, and office Olympics.
- **Pranks and Jokes:** Light-hearted pranks and jokes are a part of the daily routine, fostering a playful atmosphere.

Interactive Workstations

- **Nerf Guns and Toys:** Employees often have Nerf guns and other toys at their desks, leading to impromptu Nerf battles.
- **Massage Chairs and Napping Pods:** To help employees relax, the office includes amenities like massage chairs and napping pods.

Employee Celebrations and Recognitions

- **Hero Awards:** Employees can nominate their peers for Hero Awards, recognizing those who go above and beyond.
- **Wheel of Fortune:** Employees who perform exceptionally well might get a chance to spin the Zappos Wheel of Fortune for prizes.

Social Gatherings and Parties

- **Happy Hours:** Regular happy hours are organized to encourage socializing and team bonding outside of work.
- **Themed Parties:** Zappos holds themed parties, such as Hawaiian luaus, 80s dance parties, and more, often complete with decorations, costumes, and activities.

Creative and Unusual Perks

- **Free Food and Snacks:** The office often has free food and snacks, including occasional catered meals and treat days.
- **On-Site Petting Zoos:** Sometimes, they even bring in petting zoos or other unique attractions for employees to enjoy.

These quirky and fun activities contribute to Zappos' reputation as an exciting and enjoyable place to work, fostering a strong sense of community and employee satisfaction.

10. Sustainable and Ethical Practices

Employees increasingly value working for companies that align with their personal values, particularly concerning sustainability and ethical practices. Companies are committing to social responsibility, environmental sustainability, and ethical business practices to attract and retain employees who prioritize these values.

Case Study: Patagonia

Patagonia is committed to environmental sustainability and ethical practices, resonating with employees who value working for a company with a strong social and environmental conscience. Here are some key aspects of Patagonia's social conscience:

Environmental Activism

- **1% for the Planet:** Patagonia donates 1% of its sales to environmental organizations. This commitment has resulted in millions of dollars being contributed to grassroots environmental causes.
- **Environmental Grants:** The company provides grants to environmental groups that work to preserve and protect the environment. These grants support both local and international organizations.

Sustainable Practices

- **Sustainable Materials:** Patagonia prioritizes the use of sustainable materials such as organic cotton, recycled polyester, and hemp. They aim to minimize their environmental footprint by using materials that have a lower impact on the environment.
- **Worn Wear Program:** This program encourages customers to buy used Patagonia gear, trade in their old gear for credit, and repair damaged items. It promotes the reuse and longevity of products, reducing waste.

Fair Labor Practices

- **Fair Trade Certified:** Patagonia offers Fair Trade Certified products, ensuring that the workers who make their products receive fair wages and work in safe conditions.
- **Supply Chain Transparency:** The company is committed to transparency in its supply chain. They work closely with their suppliers to ensure fair labor practices and environmentally responsible manufacturing processes.

Corporate Activism

- **Political Engagement:** Patagonia is outspoken on political issues related to the environment. They have taken legal action against the U.S. government to protect public lands and have actively campaigned for environmental policies.
- **Climate Change Advocacy:** The company is a vocal advocate for action on climate change. They use their platform to raise awareness about the climate crisis and support policies and initiatives aimed at reducing carbon emissions.

Community Involvement

- **Volunteer Programs:** Patagonia encourages its employees to volunteer in their communities. The company offers paid time off for employees to participate in environmental and social causes.
- **Local Environmental Campaigns:** Patagonia supports local environmental campaigns through funding and resources, helping to protect local ecosystems and communities.

Innovative Environmental Initiatives

- **The Patagonia Action Works Platform**: This digital platform connects individuals with grassroots organizations working on environmental issues. It allows people to get involved in local campaigns and take action on issues they care about.
- **Regenerative Agriculture:** Patagonia is investing in regenerative agriculture practices, which aim to restore soil health, increase biodiversity, and sequester carbon. They have launched initiatives to support farmers who adopt these practices.

Corporate Responsibility

- **B Corporation Certification:** Patagonia is a certified B Corporation, meeting rigorous standards of social and environmental performance, accountability, and transparency.
- **Mission Statement:** The company's mission statement, "We're in business to save our home planet," reflects its commitment to environmental and social responsibility in all aspects of its operations.

Patagonia's social conscience is deeply integrated into its business model, influencing everything from product design and manufacturing to corporate policies and community engagement.

This commitment has established Patagonia as a leader in corporate responsibility and sustainability.

11. Technological Tools and Resources

Providing employees with the right technological tools and resources can significantly enhance their productivity and job satisfaction. Companies are investing in advanced technologies that facilitate remote work, improve communication, and streamline workflows.

Case Study: Slack

Slack offers its employees state-of-the-art tools and platforms to ensure seamless communication and collaboration, whether working remotely or in the office.

12. Transparent and Open Communication

Transparent communication fosters trust and a sense of belonging among employees. Companies are adopting open communication policies where information flows freely, and employees are kept informed about company decisions, changes, and future plans.

Case Study: Buffer

Buffer practices radical transparency, sharing everything from salaries to revenue numbers with its employees and the public, creating a culture of trust and openness.

13. Employee-Centric Leadership

Leadership plays a crucial role in ensuring workplace happiness. Companies are focusing on training leaders to be more empathetic, supportive, and employee-centric or better Ring Masters.

This involves leadership development programs, coaching, and feedback mechanisms to ensure leaders are equipped to support their teams effectively.

Case Study: Atlassian

Atlassian, the Australian software company known for products like Jira, Confluence, and Trello, has a robust leadership development program aimed at fostering the growth of its employees into strong leaders. Their leadership development programs focus on empathy, communication, and employee well-being. While specific details may vary and evolve over time, here is an overview of the typical elements found in Atlassian's leadership development initiatives:

Key Components of Atlassian's Leadership Development Program

Leadership Competency Framework

- **Skills and Behaviors:** Atlassian identifies key leadership skills and behaviors that align with its company values and business goals. These competencies often include strategic thinking, emotional intelligence, communication, and decision-making.
- **Assessment and Feedback:** Employees undergo assessments to identify their strengths and areas for improvement. Feedback is gathered from various sources, including peers, managers, and direct reports.

Training and Workshops

- **Workshops:** Regular workshops and training sessions focus on different aspects of leadership, such as conflict resolution, team management, and innovation.

- **E-learning Modules:** Online courses and resources are available for employees to learn at their own pace.

Mentorship and Coaching

- **Mentorship Programs:** Experienced leaders mentor emerging leaders, providing guidance, support, and real-world insights.
- **Executive Coaching:** Professional coaches work with leaders to develop their skills and address specific challenges.

Experiential Learning

- **Stretch Assignments:** Leaders are given challenging assignments that push them out of their comfort zones and provide opportunities to apply new skills in real-world scenarios.
- **Job Rotations:** Opportunities to work in different roles or departments to gain a broader perspective of the business.

Peer Learning and Networking:

- **Leadership Forums:** Regular forums and meetups where leaders can share experiences, challenges, and best practices.
- **Cross-functional Teams:** Collaboration across different teams to solve complex problems and innovate.

Performance Management and Career Development

- **Individual Development Plans (IDPs):** Customized plans that outline each leader's career goals and the steps needed to achieve them.
- **Continuous Feedback:** Ongoing feedback mechanisms to ensure leaders are progressing and addressing any areas of concern.

Diversity and Inclusion:

- **Inclusive Leadership Training:** Programs aimed at promoting diversity and inclusion within teams.
- **Support for Underrepresented Groups:** Specific initiatives to support the development of leaders from diverse backgrounds.

Program Goals

- **Developing Future Leaders:** Ensuring a pipeline of capable leaders who can drive Atlassian's future growth.
- **Enhancing Employee Engagement:** Engaged leaders are more effective, and their engagement positively impacts their teams.
- **Driving Innovation:** Empowering leaders to think creatively and drive innovation within the company.
- **Promoting a Positive Culture:** Cultivating a leadership style that aligns with Atlassian's core values: open company, no BS; build with heart and balance; don't "screw over" the customer; play as a team; and be the change you seek.

Atlassian's leadership development program is designed to equip its employees with the skills, knowledge, and experiences they need to become effective leaders. By focusing on a combination of training, mentorship, experiential learning, and continuous feedback, Atlassian aims to build a strong leadership culture that supports its strategic objectives and fosters a positive, inclusive workplace environment.

14. Social Connectivity and Team Building

Building strong social connections at work contributes significantly to employee happiness. Companies are organizing team-building activities, social events, and virtual meet-ups to foster camaraderie and a sense of community among employees.

Case Study: HubSpot
HubSpot organizes regular team-building activities and social events, both in-person and virtually, to strengthen social bonds and create a cohesive work environment.

15. Recognition of Individual Needs

Acknowledging and catering to individual employee needs is becoming a key focus area. Companies are implementing personalized benefits and support systems to address the unique needs of their employees, whether related to health, family, or personal development.

Case Study: Shopify
Shopify provides personalized benefits packages that allow employees to choose the benefits that best suit their individual needs, ensuring they feel supported and valued. Creating a personalized benefits package for Shopify employees involves understanding their diverse needs and preferences, ensuring a competitive edge in attracting and retaining top talent. Here's an outline of what such a benefits package might include:

Health and Wellness

- **Comprehensive Health Insurance:** Coverage for medical, dental, and vision care.
- **Mental Health Support:** Access to counseling services, therapy sessions, and mental health apps.
- **Wellness Programs:** Gym memberships, yoga classes, meditation sessions, and wellness challenges.

Financial Security

- **Competitive Salaries:** Regularly benchmarked and adjusted to remain competitive.
- **Retirement Plans:** 401(k) matching or equivalent retirement savings plans.
- **Financial Planning Services:** Access to financial advisors and planning tools.

Work-Life Balance

- **Flexible Work Hours:** Options for flexible working schedules to accommodate personal needs.
- **Remote Work Options:** Support for remote work, including necessary equipment and stipends.
- **Paid Time Off:** Generous vacation days, sick leave, and personal days.

Professional Development

- **Learning and Development:** Access to courses, workshops, and certifications.
- **Career Growth Opportunities:** Clear paths for career progression and internal mobility.
- **Mentorship Programs:** Pairing employees with mentors for guidance and support.

Family-Friendly Benefits

- **Parental Leave:** Paid leave for new parents, including maternity, paternity, and adoption leave.
- **Childcare Support:** Subsidized childcare services or on-site childcare facilities.

- **Elder Care Support:** Resources and support for employees caring for elderly family members.

Employee Recognition

- **Performance Bonuses:** Bonuses based on individual and company performance.
- **Recognition Programs:** Regular awards and recognition for outstanding contributions.
- **Milestone Celebrations:** Celebrations for work anniversaries and other significant milestones.

Lifestyle and Convenience

- **Commuter Benefits:** Subsidies for public transportation or parking.
- **On-Site Amenities:** Access to amenities such as cafeterias, relaxation spaces, and game rooms.
- **Discount Programs:** Discounts on Shopify products and services, as well as partner brands.

Social and Community Engagement

- **Volunteer Opportunities:** Paid time off for volunteering and company-organized volunteer events.
- **Employee Resource Groups:** Support for diverse employee groups and inclusion initiatives.
- **Social Events:** Regular team-building activities, company outings, and holiday parties.

Technology and Innovation

- **Latest Technology:** Providing employees with the latest devices and software for optimal productivity.
- **Innovation Time:** Allowing employees time to work on personal projects or innovative ideas.

Customization and Flexibility

To make the benefits package truly personalized, Shopify could implement a flexible benefits system where employees can choose from a variety of options to best suit their individual needs. This could include a benefits portal where employees can customize their package annually based on changing life circumstances and preferences.

By offering a comprehensive and personalized benefits package, Shopify can support its employees' diverse needs, enhance their overall well-being, and foster a positive and productive work environment.

Conclusion

Ensuring happiness in the workplace is a multifaceted endeavor that requires a holistic approach. Companies are increasingly recognizing that happy employees are key to their success and are implementing various strategies to foster a positive, supportive, and engaging work environment. By focusing on flexibility, mental health, engagement, career development, diversity, work-life balance, health, autonomy, culture, sustainability, technology, communication, leadership, social connectivity, and individual needs, companies can create workplaces where employees feel happy, valued, and motivated to contribute their best.

In the future, we can expect these trends to continue evolving, with companies constantly innovating and adapting their approaches to meet the changing needs and expectations of their workforce. As the understanding of workplace happiness deepens, businesses will be better equipped to create environments where employees thrive, leading to greater overall success and satisfaction for both employees and employers.

Reflection Questions

What three measures of ensuring happiness in the workplace resonated with you immediately?

CHAPTER 9

MEASURING HAPPINESS IN THE WORKPLACE

Measuring happiness in the workplace is critical for several reasons, as it directly impacts both employees and the organization. Here are some key points highlighting the importance of this measurement:

Employee Well-being

1. **Mental and Physical Health:** Happy employees are generally mentally and physically healthier. They experience less stress, burnout, and illness, reducing absenteeism and healthcare costs.
2. **Job Satisfaction:** Happiness is closely tied to job satisfaction. Satisfied employees are more likely to remain with the company, reducing turnover rates and the costs associated with hiring and training new staff.

Productivity and Performance

1. **Increased Productivity:** Happy employees are more engaged and motivated, leading to higher productivity levels. They are more likely to go above and beyond, contributing positively to the organization's goals.
2. **Quality of Work:** Higher levels of happiness and engagement often result in better quality work. Happy employees are more attentive, creative, and innovative, leading to improved products and services.

Organizational Culture and Climate

1. **Positive Work Environment:** Measuring and promoting happiness can help create a more positive and supportive work environment. This fosters teamwork, collaboration, and better communication among employees.
2. **Company Reputation:** Organizations prioritizing employee happiness attract and retain top talent, which enhances the company's reputation in the industry and can be a competitive advantage.

Financial Benefits

1. **Cost Savings:** Reduced turnover and absenteeism lead to significant cost savings. Moreover, higher productivity and quality work can increase the company's profitability.
2. **Customer Satisfaction:** Happy employees are likelier to provide better customer service, leading to higher customer satisfaction and loyalty, boosting sales and revenue.

Measuring Methods and Tools

There are several methods and tools available to measure workplace happiness. These range from simple surveys to more complex analytics platforms. Here are some of the most common methods and tools:

Surveys and Questionnaires

1. **Employee Satisfaction Surveys:** These surveys typically include questions about various aspects of the job, work environment, and overall satisfaction. Examples include:

   - Job Descriptive Index (JDI)
   - Minnesota Satisfaction Questionnaire (MSQ)

2. **Employee Engagement Surveys:** Focused on measuring the level of engagement, these surveys often cover areas such as job role, recognition, and alignment with company values. Examples include:

   - Gallup Q12
   - Aon Hewitt Employee Engagement Survey

3. **Pulse Surveys:** Short, frequent surveys that help track employee sentiment and happiness over time. These surveys can be administered weekly or monthly.
4. **Employee Net Promoter Score (eNPS):** This is a single-question survey asking employees how likely they are to recommend their workplace to others. It's a quick and simple way to gauge overall sentiment.

Focus Groups and Interviews

1. **Focus Groups:** Small group discussions facilitated by a moderator to gather detailed feedback on specific topics related to workplace happiness.
2. **One-on-One Interviews:** Personal interviews with employees to understand their experiences, challenges, and satisfaction levels.

Feedback Platforms and Tools

1. **Feedback Apps:** Tools that allow employees to provide continuous feedback and suggestions. Examples include:

    - Officevibe
    - TinyPulse
    - 15Five

2. **Performance Management Systems:** Platforms that integrate feedback and performance reviews, providing insights into employee happiness. Examples include:

    - Workday
    - BambooHR

3. **Recognition Platforms:** Tools that facilitate peer-to-peer recognition and reward programs, contributing to employee happiness. Examples include:
   - Bonusly
   - Kudos

Analytics and Monitoring Tools

1. **People Analytics Platforms:** Advanced tools that analyze various data points related to employee behavior and sentiment. Examples include:
   - Culture Amp
   - Glint
   - Qualtrics
2. **Sentiment Analysis:** Using artificial intelligence to analyze written feedback and communications to gauge employee sentiment.

Behavioral Observation

1. **Managerial Observations:** Managers regularly observe and note employee behaviors and interactions to gauge happiness and engagement levels.
2. **Peer Reviews:** Incorporating peer feedback to understand team dynamics and individual employee happiness.

Environmental Assessments

1. **Work Environment Assessments:** Evaluating physical workspaces and their impact on employee well-being and satisfaction.
2. **Work-life Balance Metrics:** Measure aspects such as flexible working hours, remote work options, and leave policies to understand their impact on happiness.

Gamification and Interactive Tools

1. **Gamified Surveys and Challenges:** Using game elements to make surveys more engaging and fun for employees.
2. **Wellness Apps:** Apps that track and encourage healthy behaviors contribute to employee happiness.

Combining Multiple Methods

1. **Holistic Approach:** Combining several methods to get a comprehensive view of employee happiness, such as using eNPS alongside regular pulse surveys and in-depth interviews.

By utilizing a combination of these methods and tools, organizations can gain a nuanced understanding of workplace happiness and identify specific areas for improvement.

Strategic Decision Making

1. **Informed Decisions:** Data on employee happiness helps management make informed decisions about policies, work conditions, and benefits that directly affect employee well-being.
2. **Alignment with Business Goals:** Understanding what makes employees happy enables organizations to align their business strategies with employee needs, creating a harmonious and productive work environment.

In conclusion, measuring happiness in the workplace is essential for fostering a healthy, productive, and positive organizational culture. It not only benefits employees by improving their well-being and job satisfaction but also enhances overall organizational performance and profitability.

Reflection Questions

What specific measuring tool best captures the concept of happiness in your workplace?

How can you ensure these metrics reflect both individual and collective well-being?

CHAPTER 10

THE CRITICAL ROLE OF HAPPINESS IN THE WORKPLACE

The Significance of Happiness in the Workplace

In the modern era, the workplace has evolved into more than just a venue for economic exchange; it has become a space where individuals spend a significant portion of their lives. This transformation necessitates a re-evaluation of what constitutes a successful and productive workplace. At the heart of this re-evaluation lies the concept of happiness. Happiness in the workplace is not a trivial or superficial goal; it is a critical component that can significantly influence organizational success and individual well-being.

The Multifaceted Benefits of Workplace Happiness

The benefits of fostering happiness in the workplace are multifaceted and extensive. Happy employees are more productive, creative, and engaged. They tend to exhibit higher levels of job satisfaction, leading to reduced turnover rates and lower recruitment costs. Moreover, happiness is linked to better physical and mental health, which reduces absenteeism and healthcare costs for employers. Organizations with happy employees often see improved customer satisfaction and loyalty, as content employees are more likely to provide superior service and create positive customer experiences.

From a broader perspective, workplace happiness contributes to societal well-being. When individuals are happy at work, they are more likely to experience overall life satisfaction, leading to a more harmonious and prosperous society. The ripple effects of workplace happiness extend beyond the office walls, influencing families, communities, and social structures.

The Science Behind Happiness and Productivity

Scientific research supports the notion that happiness and productivity are closely linked. Studies have shown that positive emotions enhance cognitive function, creativity, and problem-solving abilities. Happiness stimulates the release of neurotransmitters such as dopamine and serotonin, which are essential for maintaining motivation and focus. Furthermore, a positive work environment can foster collaboration and teamwork, which are critical components of a successful organization.

The field of positive psychology has extensively studied the impact of happiness on various aspects of life, including work. Researchers like Martin Seligman and Mihaly Csikszentmihalyi have demonstrated that individuals who experience positive emotions and flow states—where they are fully immersed and engaged in their tasks—tend to perform better and feel more fulfilled.

Creating a Happy Workplace: Strategies for Employers

For employers, the quest to create a happy workplace begins with a commitment to valuing and prioritizing employee well-being. Here are several strategies that employers can implement to foster happiness in the workplace:

1. **Cultivate a Positive Work Culture:** A positive work culture is characterized by mutual respect, trust, and support. Employers can cultivate such a culture by promoting open communication, recognizing and appreciating employees' contributions, and encouraging a sense of belonging.
2. **Provide Opportunities for Growth and Development:** Employees are happier when they have opportunities to learn and grow. Employers should invest in professional development programs, offer mentorship opportunities, and create clear career progression paths.
3. **Promote Work-Life Balance:** Employers should encourage employees to maintain a healthy work-life balance by offering flexible working hours, remote work options, and sufficient vacation time. Work-life balance is crucial for preventing burnout and maintaining overall well-being.

4. **Foster a Sense of Purpose:** Employees who find meaning and purpose in their work are likelier to be happy and engaged. Employers can help by clearly communicating the organization's mission and values and showing how each employee's role contributes to the overall goals.
5. **Ensure Fair Compensation and Benefits:** Fair and competitive compensation and comprehensive benefits packages are essential for employee satisfaction. Employers should regularly review and adjust salaries and benefits to ensure they meet industry standards.
6. **Support Mental and Physical Health:** Employers can promote health and well-being by providing access to wellness programs and mental health resources and encouraging healthy habits. Creating a supportive environment where employees feel comfortable discussing their health needs is also vital.
7. **Encourage Autonomy and Empowerment:** Giving employees autonomy over their work and empowering them to make decisions can enhance job satisfaction and happiness. Employers should trust their employees and provide the resources and support they need to succeed.

A Call to Action for Employers

Employers have a pivotal role in creating a workplace environment that promotes happiness. Here are concrete steps that employers can take to start this journey:

1. **Assess the Current Workplace Culture:** Conduct surveys and gather feedback to understand the current state of employee happiness and identify areas for improvement. Use this data to inform strategic initiatives.

2. **Develop a Comprehensive Happiness Strategy:** Create a strategic plan that outlines the organization's commitment to fostering happiness. This plan should include specific goals, initiatives, and metrics for measuring success.
3. **Lead by Example:** Leadership should model the behaviors and attitudes that promote happiness. Leaders who demonstrate empathy, gratitude, and positivity set the tone for the entire organization.
4. **Create a Supportive Environment:** Establish policies and practices that support employee well-being, such as flexible work arrangements, health and wellness programs, and recognition initiatives.
5. **Invest in Employee Development:** Provide resources for professional growth and development. This includes offering training programs, career development workshops, and opportunities for advancement.
6. **Foster Community and Connection:** Encourage social interaction and team-building activities that help employees build strong relationships with their colleagues.

The Role of Employees in Cultivating Happiness

While employers play a crucial role in creating a happy workplace, employees are also responsible for contributing to their own happiness and that of their colleagues. Employees should:

1. **Engage in Self-Care:** Prioritize physical and mental health by adopting healthy habits, such as regular exercise, a balanced diet, and adequate sleep. Practicing mindfulness and stress management techniques can also enhance well-being.

2. **Seek Opportunities for Growth:** Take advantage of professional development opportunities offered by your employer. Pursue additional training, certifications, and education to enhance your skills and advance in your career.
3. **Build Positive Relationships:** Foster solid and supportive relationships with colleagues. Engage in open communication, offer help and support, and participate in team-building activities.
4. **Take Initiative:** Actively contribute to creating a positive work environment by offering solutions, volunteering for projects, and participating in workplace initiatives.
5. **Communicate Needs and Feedback:** Openly communicate with managers and leaders about needs, concerns, and feedback. Constructive feedback can lead to positive changes in the workplace.
6. **Practice Gratitude and Positivity:** Cultivate a positive attitude and practice gratitude. Recognize and appreciate colleagues' efforts and contributions, and express thanks regularly.

A Collaborative Effort for a Happier Workplace

Creating a happier workplace isn't just about bean bag chairs, free snacks, and the occasional office dog (though we all know Fido helps). Creating a happy workplace is a collaborative effort that requires commitment from both employers and employees. It involves a continuous process of assessment, feedback, and improvement. By working together, employers and employees can create a work environment where happiness thrives, leading to increased productivity, engagement, and overall success. It's a collaborative effort where both employers and employees contribute to an environment that's not only productive but also genuinely enjoyable.

The Ultimate Team Effort

Creating a happier workplace is a team effort. Employers set the stage, and employees bring the energy. Together, you can create a work environment where everyone feels valued, motivated, and, yes, happy.

Conclusion

In conclusion, happiness in the workplace is not just a lofty ideal; it is a critical component of organizational and individual well-being. The benefits of a happy workplace extend beyond the office, influencing families, communities, and society as a whole. Employers and employees alike have a role to play in fostering happiness. By prioritizing well-being, creating supportive environments, and actively contributing to a positive culture, we can transform the workplace into a space where happiness and success go hand in hand. Let us take action today to build happier, healthier, and more productive workplaces for the future.

Remember, a little humor and a lot of collaboration can transform the workplace from a daily grind into a place of productivity and joy. So, let's get to it! After all, who doesn't want to enjoy their 9-to-5 with a smile and maybe a laugh or two along the way?

ABOUT THE AUTHOR

Robinson "Rob" Joseph is a distinguished leadership coach and keynote speaker renowned for his deep expertise in enhancing workplace productivity and fostering employee happiness. With over three decades of experience, Rob has dedicated his career to exploring the intricate dynamics of human behavior, motivation, and organizational success. His journey began with a keen interest in understanding what drives people to perform at their best and feel fulfilled in their professional lives.

Rob's unique approach blends scientific research with practical insights, and humor offering transformative strategies that empower leaders and teams to achieve remarkable results. His engaging and thought-provoking presentations have inspired audiences around the world, making him a sought-after speaker at conferences, corporate events, and seminars.

Rob has helped countless organizations cultivate positive work environments and unlock their full potential. His passion for helping individuals and teams thrive is evident in his personalized coaching sessions, where he provides actionable guidance tailored to each client's unique needs.

Rob holds advanced degrees in psychology, organizational behavior and leadership, further enriching his understanding of the factors that contribute to a productive and happy workplace.

When he's not coaching or speaking, Rob enjoys engaging with his community, mentoring aspiring leaders, traveling and spending time with his family. His unwavering commitment to improving the world of work has made him a respected and influential figure in the field of leadership development.

www.ingramcontent.com/pod-product-compliance
Lightning Source LLC
Chambersburg PA
CBHW071924210526
45479CB00002B/547